# PRAY THE WORD

**DISCOVERING THAT PRAYER IS NOT JUST FOR COMFORT BUT FOR RESULTS**

Jim Frease

Pray the Word
Copyright © 2018 by Joy Church International

All rights reserved. This publication may not be reproduced, distributed, or transmitted in any form or by any means, including photocopying, recording, or other electronic or mechanical methods, without the prior written permission of the publisher, except in the case of brief quotations embodied in critical reviews and certain other noncommercial uses permitted by copyright law. For permission requests, write to the publisher, addressed "Attention: Permissions Coordinator," at the address below.

Scriptures and references used in this book include both the King James Version and New King James Version of the Bible. Scripture taken from the New King James Version® is copyright © 1982 by Thomas Nelson.
Used by permission. All rights reserved.

PO Box 247
Mount Juliet, TN 37121
www.joychurch.net
Printed in the United States of America
Frease, Jim.
Pray the Word: Discovering that Prayer Is Not Just for Comfort but for Results / Jim Frease.
p. 316
ISBN 978-0-9983918-3-0
1. Christian Life   2. Scripture
First Edition
First Printing 2018

This book is dedicated to
Pastor Dave Goldner,
my executive pastor and
right-hand man for 28 years.
Your help in bringing
God's dream to pass
has been invaluable to me!

# CONTENTS

Introduction ................................................. 1
1. Why Pray the Word? ............................... 5
2. Addiction/Freedom ................................. 9
3. Adversity ............................................... 13
4. Anger .................................................... 21
5. Anxiety/Worry/Stress ............................. 25
6. Authority over the Devil ......................... 31
7. Boldness ............................................... 35
8. Character/Integrity ................................ 41
9. Children ................................................ 45
10. Confidence ........................................... 53
11. Contentment ......................................... 57
12. Depression/Joy ...................................... 59
13. Destiny/Purpose ..................................... 63
14. Direction ............................................... 67
15. Discipline/Diligence ................................ 73
16. Evangelism ............................................ 79
17. Faith ..................................................... 89
18. Faithfulness ........................................... 97
19. Favor .................................................... 101
20. Fear/Courage ........................................ 105
21. Fear of Man .......................................... 111
22. Finances ............................................... 115
23. Forgiveness ........................................... 121
24. Friends ................................................. 127
25. Grace ................................................... 131
26. Grief .................................................... 135
27. Guilt ..................................................... 141

| | |
|---|---|
| 28. Healing/Health | 145 |
| 29. Honesty | 151 |
| 30. Honor/Respect | 155 |
| 31. Hope | 159 |
| 32. Intimacy with God | 163 |
| 33. Leadership | 169 |
| 34. Loneliness | 175 |
| 35. Long Life | 179 |
| 36. Love: God's Love for Me | 183 |
| 37. Love: God's Love Toward Others | 189 |
| 38. Marriage | 193 |
| 39. Negative Thoughts | 199 |
| 40. Obedience to God | 203 |
| 41. Overcoming My Past | 209 |
| 42. Power of Our Words | 213 |
| 43. Prayer | 221 |
| 44. Praying for Those in Authority | 229 |
| 45. Pregnancy | 233 |
| 46. Pride/Humility | 239 |
| 47. Protection/Safety | 247 |
| 48. Purity | 253 |
| 49. Racism | 257 |
| 50. Selfishness | 261 |
| 51. Strength | 265 |
| 52. Thankfulness | 269 |
| 53. Unsaved Loved Ones | 273 |
| 54. Victory | 277 |
| 55. What's Taking So Long, God? | 283 |
| 56. Who You Are in Christ | 291 |
| 57. Wisdom | 297 |

# INTRODUCTION

For too long, the church has taught prayer as some sort of spiritual placebo, almost as if God pats us on our head, saying, "There, there . . . One day, when you get to Heaven, everything will be all right. In the meantime, you just be comforted and keep a good attitude while your ship is slowly sinking."

Nothing could be further from the truth!

The Bible tells us in Jeremiah 3:15, "And I will give you pastors according to mine heart, which shall feed you with knowledge and understanding." Knowledge is the "what," but understanding is the "how." If I tell you what to pray without telling you how, you'll just end up frustrated. However, as a pastor after God's heart, I want to tell you what and how to pray. That way, you'll end up motivated.

This book is not designed to be a theological manuscript on prayer. Rather, this book will help you discover the purpose and power of praying the Word. It is designed to show you how to specifically pray the Word and receive actual results!

The first chapter will give you a biblical template for praying the Word. The remaining chapters are dedicated to giving you specific verses for various situations and challenges that life may bring your way. This way, you can easily discover what and how to pray in nearly any situation you will face for the rest of your life.

Included in each chapter is a specific "Pray the Word" practical example of how to pray the Scriptures. We have also conveniently laid out the Bible verses in both the King James and New King James versions for easier understanding. Note that this book is not designed to give an exhaustive list of every verse in each subject matter. My goal in this book is not to teach you about the subject, but what to pray within each subject.

Finally, please remember that praying the Word is not a substitute for doing the Word. For example, one chapter is dedicated to character and integrity. In this chapter, we give a specific example of praying Psalm 26:11. This verse tells us to walk in our integrity. Praying it is not the same as doing it, but when you do pray the Word, two very powerful things will occur: First, your mind will be renewed (Rom. 12:2), and I've found that what you continually mind, you'll eventually find. Second, when you pray and believe the Word of God, you'll bring the power of God to this area of your life because the Word of God is alive and powerful (Heb. 4:12). Then, you won't be doing the Word in self-effort; you'll be doing it in Spirit-empowerment. You'll have to make the decision, but when you pray the Scriptures, God will bring the provision!

## Introduction

Let's begin our journey of not just praying for comfort but praying for results!

Pray the Word

# 1 Why Pray the Word?

The Bible tells us, "For we have not an high priest which cannot be touched with the feelings of our infirmities; but was in all points tempted like as we are, yet without sin. Let us therefore come boldly unto the throne of grace, that we may obtain mercy, and find grace to help in time of need" (Heb. 4:15–16). These powerful verses tell us that when Jesus was here on this earth, He was tempted in every area, just like we are, yet He successfully navigated through these temptations without sin. Therefore, we should come boldly (the Greek word *parreesia*, which means a cheerful confidence) to the throne of grace, and there we can obtain mercy and timely help for whatever we are going through. However, to come boldly and with a cheerful confidence, you must not come to the throne with your problem. Jesus already knows about your problem and has great compassion toward you. You must come in prayer with the answer, and the answers to all of life's problems can be found in the Word of God. Prayer should not be us talking to God about Earth, but God talking to us about Heaven!

The Bible tells us in John 15:7, "If ye abide in me, and my words abide in you, ye shall ask what ye will, and it shall be done unto you." At first glance, this verse appears too good to be true. This powerful verse does not say you can ask what He will, but it actually tells us you can ask what you will! However, this verse comes with what I call a "child-proof safety cap."

As you know, most medicine is not designed for children, and so it comes with a child-proof safety cap to keep children out. I actually think they should call it an adult-proof safety cap since some of them seem like they can only be opened with a sledgehammer!

Notice the word "abide." This is the Greek word *meno*, which means "to remain as a habit." When God's Word remains as a habit in my heart, I will not ask anything outside of God's Word because my will and His will are united. However, notice the direct connection to God's Word abiding in your heart and specific results to specific prayers: "it shall be done unto you."

The Bible also tells us, "And this is the confidence we have in him, that if we ask anything according to his will, he heareth us: And if we know that he hear us, whatsoever we ask, we know that we have the petitions that we desired of him" (1 Jn. 5:14–15).

Let's look at the progression in these vital verses. We have confidence in prayer when the following things take place:

1. If we ask anything according to His will, He hears us.
2. We know if He hears us, then we have the petition (prayers) we have desired of Him.

Now, some have misinterpreted these verses and assume the key to getting God to hear us is to stick the phrase "if it be Thy will" on the back of every prayer. How can that possibly give you confidence in prayer if you are not even sure what His will is?

## Why Pray the Word?

Of course, the phrase "if it be Your will" does have great value in our prayer life when we don't know His will for our lives. For example, I may not know if God wants me to take a job in Michigan or not (though as an Ohio State fan, I can tell you that He probably doesn't). Therefore, I can conclude my prayer with "if it be Thy will."

However, let me share with you 2 Corinthians 1:20: "For all the promises of God in him are yea, and in him Amen, unto the glory of God by us." This enlightening verse clearly tells us that if God has promised something, that is His "yea," His "yes." In other words, His Word is His will! Shouldn't that be the case for us as well? My word represents my will. If you tell your friends that Pastor Jim is going to pay your rent this month, you'd better be sure that I indeed said that! However, if I do say that I am going to pay your rent this month, you can take it to the bank that I will do exactly that. Why? My word is my will.

Likewise, God's Word is His will. If He promised it, that is His "yes." Now, it's up to us, according to 2 Corinthians 1:20, to give our "amen" to it. The word "amen" means "so be it." God's promise is God's "yes." However, that will do you no good until you add your "so be it" in your life.

Now, we can read 1 John 5:14-15 in a new light:

1. If we ask anything according to His will (which we can know through His Word because His Word is His will), He hears us.
2. We know if He hears us, then we have the petitions we have asked of Him. Therefore, your key to confidence in prayer is praying His Word!

Now, let's look at Hebrews 13:5–6: "Let your conversation be without covetousness; and be content with such things as ye have:

for he hath said, I will never leave thee, nor forsake thee. So that we may boldly say, The Lord is my helper, and I will not fear what man shall do unto me."

There are all kinds of things that I can share with you about these verses in context. However, I simply want to expound to you a very powerful principle that can be found in these verses. Notice the phrases "for he hath said" and "so that we may boldly say." This results in a vital prayer principle: "He hath said . . . so that we may boldly say."

It was spoken so that it could be written. Now, it is written so that it can be spoken!

Even in the Lord's Prayer, in which Jesus teaches prayer principles, He tells us, "Thy kingdom come, thy will be done in earth, as it is in heaven" (Matt. 6:10). In the Greek language, this verse is written in the command form and reads this way: "Come thy kingdom and be done thy will, on earth as it is in heaven." If I am going to adhere to Jesus' teaching and command the will of God to be done here on this earth, I'd better find out what His will is.

The Bible tells us in Jeremiah 1:12, "Then said the Lord unto me, thou hast well seen: for I will hasten my word to perform it." Notice the Bible tells us that God watches over His Word to perform it. Not our opinion, not our tradition, but His Word. The Word of God then becomes God's part of our prayer life. When you pray the Word, you are starting your prayer life with the answer and not the problem.

Now, we can plainly see: when we pray the Word, we are not praying just for comfort; we are praying for results!

# 2
## Addictions Freedom

> "Thank You, Father, that I continue in the Word, I know the truth, and the truth makes me free!"
> John 8:32

### Psalm 119:11
**KJV:** Thy word have I hid in mine heart, that I might not sin against thee.

**NKJV:** Your word I have hidden in my heart, that I might not sin against You.

### John 8:31: 32
**KJV:** Then said Jesus to those Jews which believed on him, If ye continue in my word, then are ye my disciples indeed; and ye shall know the truth, and the truth shall make you free.

**NKJV:** Then Jesus said to those Jews who believed Him, "If you abide in My word, you are My disciples indeed. And you shall know the truth, and the truth shall make you free."

### John 8:36

**KJV:** If the Son therefore shall make you free, ye shall be free indeed.

**NKJV:** Therefore if the Son makes you free, you shall be free indeed.

### Romans 6:12

**KJV:** Let not sin therefore reign in your mortal body, that ye should obey it in the lusts thereof.

**NKJV:** Therefore do not let sin reign in your mortal body, that you should obey it in its lusts.

### Romans 6:14

**KJV:** For sin shall not have dominion over you: for ye are not under the law, but under grace.

**NKJV:** For sin shall not have dominion over you, for you are not under law but under grace.

### Romans 8:2

**KJV:** For the law of the Spirit of life in Christ Jesus hath made me free from the law of sin and death.

**NKJV:** For the law of the Spirit of life in Christ Jesus has made me free from the law of sin and death.

### Romans 12:2

**KJV:** And be not conformed to this world: but be ye transformed by the renewing of your mind, that ye may prove what is that good, and acceptable, and perfect, will of God.

**NKJV:** And do not be conformed to this world, but be transformed by the renewing of your mind, that you may prove what is that good and acceptable and perfect will of God.

### 1 Corinthians 9:25–27

**KJV:** And every man that striveth for the mastery is temperate in all things. Now they do it to obtain a corruptible crown; but we an incorruptible. I therefore so run, not as uncertainly; so fight I, not as one that beateth the air: but I keep under my body, and bring it into subjection: lest that by any means, when I have preached to others, I myself should be a castaway.

**NKJV:** And everyone who competes for the prize is temperate in all things. Now they do it to obtain a perishable crown, but we for an imperishable crown. Therefore I run thus: not with uncertainty. Thus I fight: not as one who beats the air. But I discipline my body and bring it into subjection, lest, when I have preached to others, I myself should become disqualified.

### 2 Corinthians 10:5

**KJV:** Casting down imaginations, and every high thing that exalteth itself against the knowledge of God, and bringing into captivity every thought to the obedience of Christ.

**NKJV:** Casting down arguments and every high thing that exalts itself against the knowledge of God, bringing every thought into captivity to the obedience of Christ.

### Galatians 5:1

**KJV:** Stand fast therefore in the liberty wherewith Christ hath made us free, and be not entangled again with the yoke of bondage.

**NKJV:** Stand fast therefore in the liberty by which Christ has made us free, and do not be entangled again with a yoke of bondage.

### Galatians 5:16

**KJV:** This I say then, walk in the Spirit, and ye shall not fulfil the lust of the flesh.

**NKJV:** I say then: walk in the Spirit, and you shall not fulfill the lust of the flesh.

### Philippians 4:13

**KJV:** I can do all things through Christ which strengtheneth me.

**NKJV:** I can do all things through Christ who strengthens me.

### Titus 2:12

**KJV:** Teaching us that, denying ungodliness and worldly lusts, we should live soberly, righteously, and godly, in this present world.

**NKJV:** Teaching us that, denying ungodliness and worldly lusts, we should live soberly, righteously, and godly in the present age.

# 3 Adversity

> "Thank You, Father, that today
> I am more than a conqueror."
> Romans 8:37

### Deuteronomy 23:5

**KJV:** Nevertheless the Lord thy God would not hearken unto Balaam; but the Lord thy God turned the curse into a blessing unto thee, because the Lord thy God loved thee.

**NKJV:** Nevertheless the Lord your God would not listen to Balaam, but the Lord your God turned the curse into a blessing for you, because the Lord your God loves you.

### Psalm 16:8

**KJV:** I have set the Lord always before me: because he is at my right hand, I shall not be moved.

**NKJV:** I have set the Lord always before me; because He is at my right hand I shall not be moved.

### Psalm 30:11

**KJV:** Thou hast turned for me my mourning into dancing: thou hast put off my sackcloth, and girded me with gladness.

**NKJV:** You have turned for me my mourning into dancing; You have put off my sackcloth and clothed me with gladness.

### Psalm 34:4

**KJV:** I sought the Lord, and he heard me, and delivered me from all my fears.

**NKJV:** I sought the Lord, and He heard me, and delivered me from all my fears.

### Psalm 34:7

**KJV:** The angel of the Lord encampeth round about them that fear him, and delivereth them.

**NKJV:** The angel of the Lord encamps all around those who fear Him, and delivers them.

### Psalm 34:17

**KJV:** The righteous cry, and the Lord heareth, and delivereth them out of all their troubles.

**NKJV:** The righteous cry out, and the Lord hears, and delivers them out of all their troubles.

### Psalm 34:19

**KJV:** Many are the afflictions of the righteous: but the Lord delivereth him out of them all.

**NKJV:** Many are the afflictions of the righteous, but the Lord delivers him out of them all.

### Psalm 46:1

**KJV:** God is our refuge and strength, a very present help in trouble.

**NKJV:** God is our refuge and strength, a very present help in trouble.

### Psalm 86:17

**KJV:** Shew me a token for good; that they which hate me may see it, and be ashamed: because thou, Lord, hast holpen me, and comforted me.

**NKJV:** Show me a sign for good, that those who hate me may see it and be ashamed, because You, Lord, have helped me and comforted me.

### Psalm 91:14–15

**KJV:** Because he hath set his love upon me, therefore will I deliver him: I will set him on high, because he hath known my name. He shall call upon me, and I will answer him: I will be with him in trouble; I will deliver him, and honour him.

**NKJV:** Because he has set his love upon Me, therefore I will deliver him; I will set him on high, because he has known My name. He shall call upon Me, and I will answer him; I will be with him in trouble; I will deliver him and honor him.

### Psalm 107:19–20

**KJV:** Then they cry unto the Lord in their trouble, and he saveth them out of their distresses. He sent his word, and healed them, and delivered them from their destructions.

**NKJV:** Then they cried out to the Lord in their trouble, and He saved them out of their distresses. He sent His word and healed them, and delivered them from their destructions.

### Psalm 112:7–8a

**KJV:** He shall not be afraid of evil tidings: his heart is fixed, trusting in the Lord. His heart is established, he shall not be afraid.

**NKJV:** He will not be afraid of evil tidings; his heart is steadfast, trusting in the Lord. His heart is established; he will not be afraid.

### Psalm 113:7

**KJV:** He raiseth up the poor out of the dust, and lifteth the needy out of the dunghill.

**NKJV:** He raises the poor out of the dust, and lifts the needy out of the ash heap.

### Psalm 116:8

**KJV:** For thou hast delivered my soul from death, mine eyes from tears, and my feet from falling.

**NKJV:** For You have delivered my soul from death, my eyes from tears, and my feet from falling.

### Psalm 145:14

**KJV:** The Lord upholdeth all that fall, and raiseth up all those that be bowed down.

**NKJV:** The Lord upholds all who fall, and raises up all who are bowed down.

### Psalm 145:18–19

**KJV:** The Lord is nigh unto all them that call upon him, to all that call upon him in truth. He will fulfil the desire of them that fear him: he also will hear their cry, and will save them.

**NKJV:** The Lord is near to all who call upon Him, to all who call upon Him in truth. He will fulfill the desire of those who fear Him; He also will hear their cry and save them.

### Proverbs 24:16

**KJV:** For a just man falleth seven times, and riseth up again: but the wicked shall fall into mischief.

**NKJV:** For a righteous man may fall seven times and rise again, but the wicked shall fall by calamity.

### Ecclesiastes 7:14

**KJV:** In the day of prosperity be joyful, but in the day of adversity consider: God also hath set the one over against the other, to the end that man should find nothing after him.

**NKJV:** In the day of prosperity be joyful, but in the day of adversity consider: surely God has appointed the one as well as the other, so that man can find out nothing that will come after him.

### Isaiah 40:31

**KJV:** But they that wait upon the Lord shall renew their strength; they shall mount up with wings as eagles; they shall run, and not be weary; and they shall walk, and not faint.

**NKJV:** But those who wait on the Lord shall renew their strength; they shall mount up with wings like eagles, they shall run and not be weary, they shall walk and not faint.

### Isaiah 43:2

**KJV:** When thou passest through the waters, I will be with thee; and through the rivers, they shall not overflow thee: when thou walkest through the fire, thou shalt not be burned; neither shall the flame kindle upon thee.

**NKJV:** When you pass through the waters, I will be with you; and through the rivers, they shall not overflow you. When you walk through the fire, you shall not be burned, nor shall the flame scorch you.

### John 16:33

**KJV:** These things I have spoken unto you, that in me ye might have peace. In the world ye shall have tribulation: but be of good cheer; I have overcome the world.

**NKJV:** These things I have spoken to you, that in Me you may have peace. In the world you will have tribulation; but be of good cheer, I have overcome the world.

### Romans 8:37

**KJV:** Nay, in all these things we are more than conquerors through him that loved us.

**NKJV:** Yet in all these things we are more than conquerors through Him who loved us.

### 2 Corinthians 1:10

**KJV:** Who delivered us from so great a death, and doth deliver: in whom we trust that he will yet deliver us.

**NKJV:** Who delivered us from so great a death, and does deliver us; in whom we trust that He will still deliver us.

### 2 Timothy 4:17–18

**KJV:** Notwithstanding the Lord stood with me, and strengthened me; that by me the preaching might be fully known, and that all the Gentiles might hear: and I was delivered out of the mouth of the lion. And the Lord shall deliver me from every evil work, and will preserve me unto his heavenly kingdom: to whom be glory for ever and ever. Amen.

**NKJV:** But the Lord stood with me and strengthened me, so that the message might be preached fully through me, and that all the Gentiles might hear. Also I was delivered out of the mouth of the lion. And the Lord will deliver me from every evil work and preserve me for His heavenly kingdom. To Him be glory forever and ever. Amen!

Pray the Word

# 4 Anger

> "Thank You, Father, that today
> I am slow to anger."
> James 1:19

### Psalm 37:8

**KJV:** Cease from anger, and forsake wrath: fret not thyself in any wise to do evil.

**NKJV:** Cease from anger, and forsake wrath; do not fret—it only causes harm.

### Proverbs 15:1

**KJV:** A soft answer turneth away wrath: but grievous words stir up anger.

**NKJV:** A soft answer turns away wrath, but a harsh word stirs up anger.

### Proverbs 16:32

**KJV:** He that is slow to anger is better than the mighty; and he that ruleth his spirit than he that taketh a city.

**NKJV:** He who is slow to anger is better than the mighty, and he who rules his spirit than he who takes a city.

### Proverbs 17:27–28

**KJV:** He that hath knowledge spareth his words: and a man of understanding is of an excellent spirit. Even a fool, when he holdeth his peace, is counted wise: and he that shutteth his lips is esteemed a man of understanding.

**NKJV:** He who has knowledge spares his words, and a man of understanding is of a calm spirit. Even a fool is counted wise when he holds his peace; when he shuts his lips, he is considered perceptive.

### Proverbs 19:11

**KJV:** The discretion of a man deferreth his anger; and it is his glory to pass over a transgression.

**NKJV:** The discretion of a man makes him slow to anger, and his glory is to overlook a transgression.

### 1 Corinthians 13:4–5

**KJV:** Charity suffereth long, and is kind; charity envieth not; charity vaunteth not itself, is not puffed up, doth not behave itself unseemly, seeketh not her own, is not easily provoked, thinketh no evil, doth not behave itself unseemly, seeketh not her own, is not easily provoked, thinketh no evil.

**NKJV:** Love suffers long and is kind; love does not envy; love does not parade itself, is not puffed up; does not behave rudely, does not seek its own, is not provoked, thinks no evil; does not behave rudely, does not seek its own, is not provoked, thinks no evil.

### Ephesians 4:26–27

**KJV:** Let not the sun go down upon your wrath: neither give place to the devil.

**NKJV:** Do not let the sun go down on your wrath, nor give place to the devil.

### 2 Timothy 2:24

**KJV:** And the servant of the Lord must not strive; but be gentle unto all men, apt to teach, patient.

**NKJV:** And a servant of the Lord must not quarrel but be gentle to all, able to teach, patient.

### James 1:19

**KJV:** Wherefore, my beloved brethren, let every man be swift to hear, slow to speak, slow to wrath.

**NKJV:** So then, my beloved brethren, let every man be swift to hear, slow to speak, slow to wrath.

# Pray the Word

# 5 Anxiety Worry Stress

> "Thank You, Father, that today I'm not anxious for anything, and I have the peace of God that passes all understanding."
> Philippians 4:6–7

### Psalm 29:11

**KJV:** The Lord will give strength unto his people; the Lord will bless his people with peace.

**NKJV:** The Lord will give strength to His people; the Lord will bless His people with peace.

### Psalm 37:7

**KJV:** Rest in the Lord, and wait patiently for him: fret not thyself because of him who prospereth in his way, because of the man who bringeth wicked devices to pass.

**NKJV:** Rest in the Lord, and wait patiently for Him; do not fret because of him who prospers in his way, because of the man who brings wicked schemes to pass.

### Psalm 55:22

**KJV:** Cast thy burden upon the Lord, and he shall sustain thee: he shall never suffer the righteous to be moved.

**NKJV:** Cast your burden on the Lord, and He shall sustain you; He shall never permit the righteous to be moved.

### Proverbs 12:28

**KJV:** In the way of righteousness is life; and in the pathway thereof there is no death.

**NKJV:** In the way of righteousness is life, and in its pathway there is no death.

### Proverbs 14:30

**KJV:** A sound heart is the life of the flesh: but envy the rottenness of the bones.

**NKJV:** A sound heart is life to the body, but envy is rottenness to the bones.

### Proverbs 15:13

**KJV:** A merry heart maketh a cheerful countenance: but by sorrow of the heart the spirit is broken.

**NKJV:** A merry heart makes a cheerful countenance, but by sorrow of the heart the spirit is broken.

### Isaiah 26:3

**KJV:** Thou wilt keep him in perfect peace, whose mind is stayed on thee: because he trusteth in thee.

**NKJV:** You will keep him in perfect peace, whose mind is stayed on You, because he trusts in You.

### Matthew 6:31
**KJV:** Therefore take no thought, saying, what shall we eat? Or, what shall we drink? Or, wherewithal shall we be clothed?

**NKJV:** Therefore do not worry, saying, "What shall we eat?" or "What shall we drink?" or "What shall we wear?"

### Matthew 11:28–30
**KJV:** Come unto me, all ye that labour and are heavy laden, and I will give you rest. Take my yoke upon you, and learn of me; for I am meek and lowly in heart: and ye shall find rest unto your souls. For my yoke is easy, and my burden is light.

**NKJV:** Come to Me, all you who labor and are heavy laden, and I will give you rest. Take My yoke upon you and learn from Me, for I am gentle and lowly in heart, and you will find rest for your souls. For My yoke is easy and My burden is light.

### John 14:1
**KJV:** Let not your heart be troubled: ye believe in God, believe also in me.

**NKJV:** Let not your heart be troubled; you believe in God, believe also in Me.

### John 14:27
**KJV:** Peace I leave with you, my peace I give unto you: not as the world giveth, give I unto you. Let not your heart be troubled, neither let it be afraid.

**NKJV:** Peace I leave with you, my peace I give to you; not as the world gives do I give to you. Let not your heart be troubled, neither let it be afraid.

### Romans 14:17

**KJV:** For the kingdom of God is not meat and drink; but righteousness, and peace, and joy in the Holy Ghost.

**NKJV:** For the kingdom of God is not eating and drinking, but righteousness and peace and joy in the Holy Spirit.

### Romans 15:13

**KJV:** Now the God of hope fill you with all joy and peace in believing, that ye may abound in hope, through the power of the Holy Ghost.

**NKJV:** Now may the God of hope fill you with all joy and peace in believing, that you may abound in hope by the power of the Holy Spirit.

### 2 Corinthians 10:5

**KJV:** Casting down imaginations, and every high thing that exalteth itself against the knowledge of God, and bringing into captivity every thought to the obedience of Christ.

**NKJV:** Casting down arguments and every high thing that exalts itself against the knowledge of God, bringing every thought into captivity to the obedience of Christ.

### Philippians 4:6–7

**KJV:** Be careful for nothing; but in every thing by prayer and supplication with thanksgiving let your requests be made known unto God. And the peace of God, which passeth all understanding, shall keep your hearts and minds through Christ Jesus.

Anxiety | Worry | Stress

**NKJV:** Be anxious for nothing, but in everything by prayer and supplication, with thanksgiving, let your requests be made known to God; and the peace of God, which surpasses all understanding, will guard your hearts and minds through Christ Jesus.

### 1 Peter 5:7

**KJV:** Casting all your care upon him; for he careth for you.

**NKJV:** Casting all your care upon Him, for He cares for you.

## Pray the Word

# 6 Authority over the Devil

> "Thank You, Father, that I submit myself to You today. I resist the devil, and he shall flee from me."
> James 4:7

### Matthew 10:1

**KJV:** And when he had called unto him his twelve disciples, he gave them power against unclean spirits, to cast them out, and to heal all manner of sickness and all manner of disease.

**NKJV:** And when He had called His twelve disciples to Him, He gave them power over unclean spirits, to cast them out, and to heal all kinds of sickness and all kinds of disease.

### Luke 10:19

**KJV:** Behold, I give unto you power to tread on serpents and scorpions, and over all the power of the enemy: and nothing shall by any means hurt you.

**NKJV:** Behold, I give you the authority to trample on serpents and scorpions, and over all the power of the enemy, and nothing shall by any means hurt you.

### Romans 5:17

**KJV:** For if by one man's offence death reigned by one; much more they which receive abundance of grace and of the gift of righteousness shall reign in life by one, Jesus Christ.

**NKJV:** For if by the one man's offense death reigned through the one, much more those who receive abundance of grace and of the gift of righteousness will reign in life through the One, Jesus Christ.

### Romans 16:20

**KJV:** And the God of peace shall bruise Satan under your feet shortly. The grace of our Lord Jesus Christ be with you. Amen.

**NKJV:** And the God of peace will crush Satan under your feet shortly. The grace of our Lord Jesus Christ be with you. Amen.

### Ephesians 1:19–23

**KJV:** And what is the exceeding greatness of his power to us-ward who believe, according to the working of his mighty power, which he wrought in Christ, when he raised him from the dead, and set him at his own right hand in the heavenly places, far above all principality, and power, and might, and dominion, and every name that is named, not only in this world, but also in that which is to come: and hath put all things under his feet, and gave him to be the head over all things to the church, which is his body, the fulness of him that filleth all in all.

**NKJV:** And what is the exceeding greatness of His power toward us who believe, according to the working of His mighty power which He worked in Christ when He raised Him from the dead and seated Him at His right hand in the heavenly places, far above all principality and power and might and dominion, and every name that is named, not only in this age but also in that which is to come. And He put all things under His feet, and gave Him to be head over all things to the church, which is His body, the fullness of Him who fills all in all.

### Ephesians 6:10

**KJV:** Finally, my brethren, be strong in the Lord, and in the power of his might.

**NKJV:** Finally, my brethren, be strong in the Lord and in the power of His might.

### Ephesians 6:16

**KJV:** Above all, taking the shield of faith, wherewith ye shall be able to quench all the fiery darts of the wicked.

**NKJV:** Above all, taking the shield of faith with which you will be able to quench all the fiery darts of the wicked one.

### Colossians 1:13

**KJV:** Who hath delivered us from the power of darkness, and hath translated us into the kingdom of his dear Son.

**NKJV:** He has delivered us from the power of darkness and conveyed us into the kingdom of the Son of His love.

### Colossians 2:10

**KJV:** And ye are complete in him, which is the head of all principality and power.

**NKJV:** And you are complete in Him, who is the head of all principality and power.

## James 4:7

**KJV:** Submit yourselves therefore to God. Resist the devil, and he will flee from you.

**NKJV:** Therefore submit to God. Resist the devil and he will flee from you.

## 1 John 4:4

**KJV:** Ye are of God, little children, and have overcome them: because greater is he that is in you, than he that is in the world.

**NKJV:** You are of God, little children, and have overcome them, because He who is in you is greater than he who is in the world.

# 7 Boldness

> "Thank You, Father, that today
> I'm as bold as a lion."
> Proverbs 28:1

### Psalm 27:14

**KJV:** Wait on the Lord: be of good courage, and he shall strengthen thine heart: wait, I say, on the Lord.

**NKJV:** Wait on the Lord; be of good courage, and He shall strengthen your heart; wait, I say, on the Lord!

### Proverbs 28:1

**KJV:** The wicked flee when no man pursueth: but the righteous are bold as a lion.

**NKJV:** The wicked flee when no one pursues, but the righteous are bold as a lion.

## Pray the Word

### Matthew 5:14–16

**KJV:** Ye are the light of the world. A city that is set on an hill cannot be hid. Neither do men light a candle, and put it under a bushel, but on a candlestick; and it giveth light unto all that are in the house. Let your light so shine before men, that they may see your good works, and glorify your Father which is in heaven.

**NKJV:** You are the light of the world. A city that is set on a hill cannot be hidden. Nor do they light a lamp and put it under a basket, but on a lampstand, and it gives light to all who are in the house. Let your light so shine before men, that they may see your good works and glorify your Father in heaven.

### Acts 4:13

**KJV:** Now when they saw the boldness of Peter and John, and perceived that they were unlearned and ignorant men, they marvelled; and they took knowledge of them, that they had been with Jesus.

**NKJV:** Now when they saw the boldness of Peter and John, and perceived that they were uneducated and untrained men, they marveled. And they realized that they had been with Jesus.

### Acts 4:29

**KJV:** And now, Lord, behold their threatenings: and grant unto thy servants, that with all boldness they may speak thy word.

**NKJV:** Now, Lord, look on their threats, and grant to Your servants that with all boldness they may speak Your word,

### Acts 4:31

**KJV:** And when they had prayed, the place was shaken where they were assembled together; and they were all filled with the Holy Ghost, and they spake the word of God with boldness.

**NKJV:** And when they had prayed, the place where they were assembled together was shaken; and they were all filled with the Holy Spirit, and they spoke the word of God with boldness.

### Romans 1:16a

**KJV:** For I am not ashamed of the gospel of Christ: for it is the power of God unto salvation to every one that believeth.

**NKJV:** For I am not ashamed of the gospel of Christ, for it is the power of God to salvation for everyone who believes.

### Romans 8:31

**KJV:** What shall we then say to these things? If God be for us, who can be against us?

**NKJV:** What then shall we say to these things? If God is for us, who can be against us?

### Ephesians 3:12

**KJV:** In whom we have boldness and access with confidence by the faith of him.

**NKJV:** In whom we have boldness and access with confidence through faith in Him.

### Ephesians 6:19–20

**KJV:** And for me, that utterance may be given unto me, that I may open my mouth boldly, to make known the mystery of the gospel, for which I am an ambassador in bonds: that therein I may speak boldly, as I ought to speak.

**NKJV:** And for me, that utterance may be given to me, that I may open my mouth boldly to make known the mystery of the gospel, for which I am an ambassador in chains; that in it I may speak boldly, as I ought to speak.

### Philippians 4:13

**KJV:** I can do all things through Christ which strengtheneth me.

**NKJV:** I can do all things through Christ who strengthens me.

### 2 Timothy 1:7

**KJV:** For God hath not given us the spirit of fear; but of power, and of love, and of a sound mind.

**NKJV:** For God has not given us a spirit of fear, but of power and of love and of a sound mind.

### Hebrews 4:16

**KJV:** Let us therefore come boldly unto the throne of grace, that we may obtain mercy, and find grace to help in time of need.

**NKJV:** Let us therefore come boldly to the throne of grace, that we may obtain mercy and find grace to help in time of need.

### Hebrews 10:19

**KJV:** Having therefore, brethren, boldness to enter into the holiest by the blood of Jesus.

**NKJV:** Therefore, brethren, having boldness to enter the Holiest by the blood of Jesus.

### Hebrews 13:5–6

**KJV:** Let your conversation be without covetousness; and be content with such things as ye have: for he hath said, I will never leave thee, nor forsake thee. So that we may boldly say, The Lord is my helper, and I will not fear what man shall do unto me.

## Boldness

**NKJV:** Let your conduct be without covetousness; be content with such things as you have. For He Himself has said, "I will never leave you nor forsake you." So we may boldly say: "The Lord is my helper; I will not fear. What can man do to me?"

Pray the Word

# 8 Character Integrity

> "Thank You, Father, that today
> I walk in my integrity."
> Psalm 26:11

### Psalm 15:4

**KJV:** In whose eyes a vile person is contemned; but he honoureth them that fear the LORD. He that sweareth to his own hurt, and changeth not.

**NKJV:** In whose eyes a vile person is despised, but he honors those who fear the LORD; He who swears to his own hurt and does not change.

### Psalm 25:21

**KJV:** Let integrity and uprightness preserve me; for I wait on thee.

**NKJV:** Let integrity and uprightness preserve me, for I wait for You.

### Psalm 26:11

**KJV:** But as for me, I will walk in mine integrity: redeem me, and be merciful unto me.

**NKJV:** But as for me, I will walk in my integrity; redeem me and be merciful to me.

### Psalm 41:12

**KJV:** And as for me, thou upholdest me in mine integrity, and settest me before thy face for ever.

**NKJV:** As for me, You uphold me in my integrity, and set me before Your face forever.

### Psalm 119:1

**KJV:** Blessed are the undefiled in the way, who walk in the law of the Lord.

**NKJV:** Blessed are the undefiled in the way, who walk in the law of the Lord!

### Proverbs 11:3

**KJV:** The integrity of the upright shall guide them: but the perverseness of transgressors shall destroy them.

**NKJV:** The integrity of the upright will guide them, but the perversity of the unfaithful will destroy them.

### Proverbs 12:4

**KJV:** A virtuous woman is a crown to her husband: but she that maketh ashamed is as rottenness in his bones.

**NKJV:** An excellent wife is the crown of her husband, but she who causes shame is like rottenness in his bones.

## Proverbs 20:7

**KJV:** The just man walketh in his integrity: his children are blessed after him.

**NKJV:** The righteous man walks in his integrity; his children are blessed after him.

## Proverbs 22:1

**KJV:** A good name is rather to be chosen than great riches, and loving favour rather than silver and gold.

**NKJV:** A good name is to be chosen rather than great riches, loving favor rather than silver and gold.

## Acts 17:11

**KJV:** These were more noble than those in Thessalonica, in that they received the word with all readiness of mind, and searched the scriptures daily, whether those things were so.

**NKJV:** These were more fair-minded than those in Thessalonica, in that they received the word with all readiness, and searched the Scriptures daily to find out whether these things were so.

## Acts 24:16

**KJV:** And herein do I exercise myself, to have always a conscience void of offence toward God, and toward men.

**NKJV:** This being so, I myself always strive to have a conscience without offense toward God and men.

## 2 Corinthians 1:12

**KJV:** For our rejoicing is this, the testimony of our conscience, that in simplicity and godly sincerity, not with fleshly wisdom, but by the grace of God, we have had our conversation in the world, and more abundantly to you-ward.

**NKJV:** For our boasting is this: the testimony of our conscience that we conducted ourselves in the world in simplicity and godly sincerity, not with fleshly wisdom but by the grace of God, and more abundantly toward you.

### 2 Corinthians 2:17

**KJV:** For we are not as many, which corrupt the word of God: but as of sincerity, but as of God, in the sight of God speak we in Christ.

**NKJV:** For we are not, as so many, peddling the word of God; but as of sincerity, but as from God, we speak in the sight of God in Christ.

### Titus 2:14

**KJV:** Who gave himself for us, that he might redeem us from all iniquity, and purify unto himself a peculiar people, zealous of good works.

**NKJV:** Who gave Himself for us, that He might redeem us from every lawless deed and purify for Himself His own special people, zealous for good works.

### 2 Peter 1:5

**KJV:** And beside this, giving all diligence, add to your faith virtue; and to virtue knowledge.

**NKJV:** But also for this very reason, giving all diligence, add to your faith virtue, to virtue knowledge.

# 9 Children

> "Thank You, Father, that great is
> the peace of my children
> for they are taught of the Lord."
> Isaiah 54:13

### Genesis 18:19

**KJV:** For I know him, that he will command his children and his household after him, and they shall keep the way of the Lord, to do justice and judgment; that the Lord may bring upon Abraham that which he hath spoken of him.

**NKJV:** For I have known him, in order that he may command his children and his household after him, that they keep the way of the Lord, to do righteousness and justice, that the Lord may bring to Abraham what He has spoken to him.

### Exodus 20:12

**KJV:** Honour thy father and thy mother: that thy days may be long upon the land which the Lord thy God giveth thee.

**NKJV:** Honor your father and your mother, that your days may be long upon the land which the Lord your God is giving you.

### Deuteronomy 6:7

**KJV:** And thou shalt teach them diligently unto thy children, and shalt talk of them when thou sittest in thine house, and when thou walkest by the way, and when thou liest down, and when thou risest up.

**NKJV:** You shall teach them diligently to your children, and shall talk of them when you sit in your house, when you walk by the way, when you lie down, and when you rise up.

### Deuteronomy 11:19

**KJV:** And ye shall teach them your children, speaking of them when thou sittest in thine house, and when thou walkest by the way, when thou liest down, and when thou risest up.

**NKJV:** You shall teach them to your children, speaking of them when you sit in your house, when you walk by the way, when you lie down, and when you rise up.

### Psalm 34:11

**KJV:** Come, ye children, hearken unto me: I will teach you the fear of the Lord.

**NKJV:** Come, you children, listen to me; I will teach you the fear of the Lord.

### Psalm 127:3–5

**KJV:** Lo, children are an heritage of the Lord: and the fruit of the womb is his reward. As arrows are in the hand of a mighty man; so are children of the youth. Happy is the man that hath his quiver full of them: they shall not be ashamed, but they shall speak with the enemies in the gate.

**NKJV:** Behold, children are a heritage from the Lord, the fruit of the womb is a reward. Like arrows in the hand of a warrior, so are the children of one's youth. Happy is the man who has his quiver full of them; they shall not be ashamed, but shall speak with their enemies in the gate.

## Proverbs 10:1

**KJV:** A wise son maketh a glad father: but a foolish son is the heaviness of his mother.

**NKJV:** A wise son makes a glad father, but a foolish son is the grief of his mother.

## Proverbs 22:6

**KJV:** Train up a child in the way he should go: and when he is old, he will not depart from it.

**NKJV:** Train up a child in the way he should go, and when he is old he will not depart from it.

## Proverbs 22:15

**KJV:** Foolishness is bound in the heart of a child; but the rod of correction shall drive it far from him.

**NKJV:** Foolishness is bound up in the heart of a child; the rod of correction will drive it far from him.

## Proverbs 23:13

**KJV:** Withhold not correction from the child: for if thou beatest him with the rod, he shall not die.

**NKJV:** Do not withhold correction from a child, for if you beat him with a rod, he will not die.

### Proverbs 23:26

**KJV:** My son, give me thine heart, and let thine eyes observe my ways.

**NKJV:** My son, give me your heart, and let your eyes observe my ways.

### Isaiah 54:13

**KJV:** And all thy children shall be taught of the Lord; and great shall be the peace of thy children.

**NKJV:** All your children shall be taught by the Lord, and great shall be the peace of your children.

### Matthew 18:2–5

**KJV:** And Jesus called a little child unto him, and set him in the midst of them, and said, Verily I say unto you, except ye be converted, and become as little children, ye shall not enter into the kingdom of heaven. Whosoever therefore shall humble himself as this little child, the same is greatest in the kingdom of heaven. And whoso shall receive one such little child in my name receiveth me.

**NKJV:** Then Jesus called a little child to Him, set him in the midst of them, and said, "Assuredly, I say to you, unless you are converted and become as little children, you will by no means enter the kingdom of heaven. Therefore whoever humbles himself as this little child is the greatest in the kingdom of heaven. Whoever receives one little child like this in My name receives Me."

### Matthew 21:15–16

**KJV:** And when the chief priests and scribes saw the wonderful things that he did, and the children crying in the temple, and saying, Hosanna to the Son of David; they were sore displeased, and said unto him,

Hearest thou what these say? And Jesus saith unto them, Yea; have ye never read, out of the mouth of babes and sucklings thou hast perfected praise?

**NKJV:** But when the chief priests and scribes saw the wonderful things that He did, and the children crying out in the temple and saying, "Hosanna to the Son of David!" They were indignant and said to Him, "Do You hear what these are saying?" And Jesus said to them, "Yes. Have you never read, 'Out of the mouth of babes and nursing infants You have perfected praise'?"

### Mark 10:13–16

**KJV:** And they brought young children to him, that he should touch them: and his disciples rebuked those that brought them. But when Jesus saw it, he was much displeased, and said unto them, Suffer the little children to come unto me, and forbid them not: for of such is the kingdom of God. Verily I say unto you, whosoever shall not receive the kingdom of God as a little child, he shall not enter therein. And he took them up in his arms, put his hands upon them, and blessed them.

**NKJV:** Then they brought little children to Him, that He might touch them; but the disciples rebuked those who brought them. But when Jesus saw it, He was greatly displeased and said to them, "Let the little children come to Me, and do not forbid them; for of such is the kingdom of God. Assuredly, I say to you, whoever does not receive the kingdom of God as a little child will by no means enter it." And He took them up in His arms, laid His hands on them, and blessed them.

### Luke 2:40

**KJV:** And the child grew, and waxed strong in spirit, filled with wisdom: and the grace of God was upon him.

**NKJV:** And the Child grew and became strong in spirit, filled with wisdom; and the grace of God was upon Him.

### Luke 2:52

**KJV:** And Jesus increased in wisdom and stature, and in favour with God and man.

**NKJV:** And Jesus increased in wisdom and stature, and in favor with God and men.

### Ephesians 6:1–4

**KJV:** Children, obey your parents in the Lord: for this is right. Honour thy father and mother; (which is the first commandment with promise;) that it may be well with thee, and thou mayest live long on the earth. And, ye fathers, provoke not your children to wrath: but bring them up in the nurture and admonition of the Lord.

**NKJV:** Children, obey your parents in the Lord, for this is right. "Honor your father and mother," which is the first commandment with promise: "that it may be well with you and you may live long on the earth." And you, fathers, do not provoke your children to wrath, but bring them up in the training and admonition of the Lord.

### Colossians 3:20

**KJV:** Children, obey your parents in all things: for this is well pleasing unto the Lord.

**NKJV:** Children, obey your parents in all things, for this is well pleasing to the Lord.

### 2 Timothy 3:15

**KJV:** And that from a child thou hast known the holy scriptures, which are able to make thee wise unto salvation through faith which is in Christ Jesus.

**NKJV:** And that from childhood you have known the Holy Scriptures, which are able to make you wise for salvation through faith which is in Christ Jesus.

### 3 John 4

**KJV:** I have no greater joy than to hear that my children walk in truth.

**NKJV:** I have no greater joy than to hear that my children walk in truth.

Pray the Word

# 10 Confidence

> "Thank You, Father, that I don't cast away my confidence, which has great recompense of reward."
> Hebrews 10:35

### Psalm 20:7

**KJV:** Some trust in chariots, and some in horses: but we will remember the name of the LORD our God.

**NKJV:** Some trust in chariots, and some in horses; but we will remember the name of the LORD our God.

### Proverbs 3:26

**KJV:** For the LORD shall be thy confidence, and shall keep thy foot from being taken.

**NKJV:** For the Lord will be your confidence, and will keep your foot from being caught.

### Isaiah 32:17

**KJV:** And the work of righteousness shall be peace; and the effect of righteousness quietness and assurance for ever.

**NKJV:** The work of righteousness will be peace, and the effect of righteousness, quietness and assurance forever.

### Jeremiah 17:7

**KJV:** Blessed is the man that trusteth in the Lord, and whose hope the Lord is.

**NKJV:** Blessed is the man who trusts in the Lord, and whose hope is the Lord.

### 1 Corinthians 15:58

**KJV:** Therefore, my beloved brethren, be ye stedfast, unmoveable, always abounding in the work of the Lord, forasmuch as ye know that your labour is not in vain in the Lord.

**NKJV:** Therefore, my beloved brethren, be steadfast, immovable, always abounding in the work of the Lord, knowing that your labor is not in vain in the Lord.

### Philippians 1:6

**KJV:** Being confident of this very thing, that he which hath begun a good work in you will perform it until the day of Jesus Christ.

**NKJV:** Being confident of this very thing, that He who has begun a good work in you will complete it until the day of Jesus Christ.

## Confidence

### Philippians 3:3

**KJV:** For we are the circumcision, which worship God in the spirit, and rejoice in Christ Jesus, and have no confidence in the flesh.

**NKJV:** For we are the circumcision, who worship God in the Spirit, rejoice in Christ Jesus, and have no confidence in the flesh,

### Philippians 4:13

**KJV:** I can do all things through Christ which strengtheneth me.

**NKJV:** I can do all things through Christ who strengthens me.

### Hebrews 10:35

**KJV:** Cast not away therefore your confidence, which hath great recompence of reward.

**NKJV:** Therefore do not cast away your confidence, which has great reward.

### 1 John 4:17

**KJV:** Herein is our love made perfect, that we may have boldness in the day of judgment: because as he is, so are we in this world.

**NKJV:** Love has been perfected among us in this: that we may have boldness in the day of judgment; because as He is, so are we in this world.

### 1 John 5:14–15

**KJV:** And this is the confidence that we have in him, that, if we ask any thing according to his will, he heareth us: and if we know that he hear us, whatsoever we ask, we know that we have the petitions that we desired of him.

**NKJV:** Now this is the confidence that we have in Him, that if we ask anything according to His will, He hears us. And if we know that He hears us, whatever we ask, we know that we have the petitions that we have asked of Him.

# 11 Contentment

> "Thank You, Father, that today I rest in the LORD and wait patiently for Him."
> Psalm 37:7

### Psalm 37:3

**KJV:** Trust in the LORD, and do good; so shalt thou dwell in the land, and verily thou shalt be fed.

**NKJV:** Trust in the LORD, and do good; dwell in the land, and feed on His faithfulness.

### Psalm 37:7

**KJV:** Rest in the LORD, and wait patiently for him: fret not thyself because of him who prospereth in his way, because of the man who bringeth wicked devices to pass.

**NKJV:** Rest in the LORD, and wait patiently for Him; do not fret because of him who prospers in his way, because of the man who brings wicked schemes to pass.

### Luke 12:15

**KJV:** And he said unto them, Take heed, and beware of covetousness: for a man's life consisteth not in the abundance of the things which he possesseth.

**NKJV:** And He said to them, "Take heed and beware of covetousness, for one's life does not consist in the abundance of the things he possesses."

### Philippians 4:11

**KJV:** Not that I speak in respect of want: for I have learned, in whatsoever state I am, therewith to be content.

**NKJV:** Not that I speak in regard to need, for I have learned in whatever state I am, to be content.

### 1 Timothy 6:6

**KJV:** But godliness with contentment is great gain.

**NKJV:** Now godliness with contentment is great gain.

### Hebrews 13:5–6

**KJV:** Let your conversation be without covetousness; and be content with such things as ye have: for he hath said, I will never leave thee, nor forsake thee. So that we may boldly say, The Lord is my helper, and I will not fear what man shall do unto me.

**NKJV:** Let your conduct be without covetousness; be content with such things as you have. For He Himself has said, "I will never leave you nor forsake you." So we may boldly say: "The Lord is my helper; I will not fear. What can man do to me?"

# 12

## Depression
## Joy

> "Thank You, Father, that this is the day the Lord has made. I WILL rejoice and be glad in it!"
> Psalm 118:24

### Psalm 16:11

**KJV:** Thou wilt shew me the path of life: in thy presence is fulness of joy; at thy right hand there are pleasures for evermore.

**NKJV:** You will show me the path of life; in Your presence is fullness of joy; at Your right hand are pleasures forevermore.

### Psalm 40:16

**KJV:** Let all those that seek thee rejoice and be glad in thee: let such as love thy salvation say continually, The Lord be magnified.

**NKJV:** Let all those who seek You rejoice and be glad in You; let such as love Your salvation say continually, "The LORD be magnified!"

## Psalm 103:1–5

**KJV:** Bless the LORD, O my soul: and all that is within me, bless his holy name. Bless the LORD, O my soul, and forget not all his benefits: who forgiveth all thine iniquities; who healeth all thy diseases; who redeemeth thy life from destruction; who crowneth thee with lovingkindness and tender mercies; who satisfieth thy mouth with good things; so that thy youth is renewed like the eagle's.

**NKJV:** Bless the LORD, O my soul; and all that is within me, bless His holy name! Bless the LORD, O my soul, and forget not all His benefits: who forgives all your iniquities, who heals all your diseases, who redeems your life from destruction, who crowns you with lovingkindness and tender mercies, who satisfies your mouth with good things, so that your youth is renewed like the eagle's.

## Psalm 118:24

**KJV:** This is the day which the LORD hath made; we will rejoice and be glad in it.

**NKJV:** This is the day the LORD has made; we will rejoice and be glad in it.

## Proverbs 15:13

**KJV:** A merry heart maketh a cheerful countenance: but by sorrow of the heart the spirit is broken.

**NKJV:** A merry heart makes a cheerful countenance, but by sorrow of the heart the spirit is broken.

## Depression | Joy

### John 15:11

**KJV:** These things have I spoken unto you, that my joy might remain in you, and that your joy might be full.

**NKJV:** These things I have spoken to you, that My joy may remain in you, and that your joy may be full.

### John 16:22

**KJV:** And ye now therefore have sorrow: but I will see you again, and your heart shall rejoice, and your joy no man taketh from you.

**NKJV:** Therefore you now have sorrow; but I will see you again and your heart will rejoice, and your joy no one will take from you.

### John 16:24

**KJV:** Hitherto have ye asked nothing in my name: ask, and ye shall receive, that your joy may be full.

**NKJV:** Until now you have asked nothing in My name. Ask, and you will receive, that your joy may be full.

### Romans 14:17

**KJV:** For the kingdom of God is not meat and drink; but righteousness, and peace, and joy in the Holy Ghost.

**NKJV:** For the kingdom of God is not eating and drinking, but righteousness and peace and joy in the Holy Spirit.

### Romans 15:13

**KJV:** Now the God of hope fill you with all joy and peace in believing, that ye may abound in hope, through the power of the Holy Ghost.

**NKJV:** Now may the God of hope fill you with all joy and peace in believing, that you may abound in hope by the power of the Holy Spirit.

### Philippians 4:4

**KJV:** Rejoice in the Lord alway: and again I say, rejoice.

**NKJV:** Rejoice in the Lord always. Again I will say, rejoice!

### 1 Thessalonians 5:16

**KJV:** Rejoice evermore.

**NKJV:** Rejoice always.

### James 1:2–4

**KJV:** My brethren, count it all joy when ye fall into divers temptations; Knowing this, that the trying of your faith worketh patience. But let patience have her perfect work, that ye may be perfect and entire, wanting nothing.

**NKJV:** My brethren, count it all joy when you fall into various trials, nowing that the testing of your faith produces patience. But let patience have its perfect work, that you may be perfect and complete, lacking nothing.

### 1 Peter 1:8

**KJV:** Whom having not seen, ye love; in whom, though now ye see him not, yet believing, ye rejoice with joy unspeakable and full of glory.

**NKJV:** Whom having not seen you love. Though now you do not see Him, yet believing, you rejoice with joy inexpressible and full of glory.

### 1 John 1:4

**KJV:** And these things write we unto you, that your joy may be full.

**NKJV:** And these things we write to you that your joy may be full.

# 13 Destiny Purpose

> "Thank You, Father, that You know Your plans for me, plans of good and not evil, to give me a future and a hope."
> Jeremiah 29:11

### 2 Chronicles 16:9

**KJV:** For the eyes of the Lord run to and fro throughout the whole earth, to shew himself strong in the behalf of them whose heart is perfect toward him. Herein thou hast done foolishly: therefore from henceforth thou shalt have wars.

**NKJV:** For the eyes of the Lord run to and fro throughout the whole earth, to show Himself strong on behalf of those whose heart is loyal to Him. In this you have done foolishly; therefore from now on you shall have wars.

### Psalm 90:12

**KJV:** So teach us to number our days, that we may apply our hearts unto wisdom.

**NKJV:** So teach us to number our days, that we may gain a heart of wisdom.

### Psalm 138:8

**KJV:** The LORD will perfect that which concerneth me: thy mercy, O LORD, endureth for ever: forsake not the works of thine own hands.

**NKJV:** The LORD will perfect that which concerns me; Your mercy, O LORD, endures forever; do not forsake the works of Your hands.

### Proverbs 16:3

**KJV:** Commit thy works unto the LORD, and thy thoughts shall be established.

**NKJV:** Commit your works to the LORD, and your thoughts will be established.

### Proverbs 19:21

**KJV:** There are many devices in a man's heart; nevertheless the counsel of the LORD, that shall stand.

**NKJV:** There are many plans in a man's heart, nevertheless the LORD's counsel—that will stand.

### Isaiah 46:10

**KJV:** Declaring the end from the beginning, and from ancient times the things that are not yet done, saying, My counsel shall stand, and I will do all my pleasure.

**NKJV:** Declaring the end from the beginning, and from ancient times things that are not yet done, saying, "My counsel shall stand, and I will do all My pleasure."

### Jeremiah 29:11

**KJV:** For I know the thoughts that I think toward you, saith the LORD, thoughts of peace, and not of evil, to give you an expected end.

**NKJV:** For I know the thoughts that I think toward you, says the LORD, thoughts of peace and not of evil, to give you a future and a hope.

### Jeremiah 33:3

**KJV:** Call unto me, and I will answer thee, and shew thee great and mighty things, which thou knowest not.

**NKJV:** Call to Me, and I will answer you, and show you great and mighty things, which you do not know.

### Habakkuk 2:2

**KJV:** And the LORD answered me, and said, Write the vision, and make it plain upon tables, that he may run that readeth it.

**NKJV:** Then the LORD answered me and said: "Write the vision and make it plain on tablets, that he may run who reads it."

### John 4:34

**KJV:** Jesus saith unto them, My meat is to do the will of him that sent me, and to finish his work.

**NKJV:** Jesus said to them, "My food is to do the will of Him who sent Me, and to finish His work."

### Romans 8:29

**KJV:** For whom he did foreknow, he also did predestinate to be conformed to the image of his Son, that he might be the firstborn among many brethren.

**NKJV:** For whom He foreknew, He also predestined to be conformed to the image of His Son, that He might be the firstborn among many brethren.

### 1 Corinthians 2:9–10a

**KJV:** But as it is written, Eye hath not seen, nor ear heard, neither have entered into the heart of man, the things which God hath prepared for them that love him. But God hath revealed them unto us by his Spirit.

**NKJV:** But as it is written: "Eye has not seen, nor ear heard, nor have entered into the heart of man the things which God has prepared for those who love Him." But God has revealed them to us through His Spirit.

### Ephesians 2:10

**KJV:** For we are his workmanship, created in Christ Jesus unto good works, which God hath before ordained that we should walk in them.

**NKJV:** For we are His workmanship, created in Christ Jesus for good works, which God prepared beforehand that we should walk in them.

# 14 Direction

> "Thank You, Father, that I am filled with the knowledge of Your will in all wisdom and spiritual understanding."
> Colossians 1:9

### Psalm 25:4–5

**KJV:** Shew me thy ways, O Lord; teach me thy paths. Lead me in thy truth, and teach me: for thou art the God of my salvation; on thee do I wait all the day.

**NKJV:** Show me Your ways, O Lord; teach me Your paths. Lead me in Your truth and teach me, for You are the God of my salvation; on You I wait all the day.

### Psalm 27:11

**KJV:** Teach me thy way, O Lord, and lead me in a plain path, because of mine enemies.

**NKJV:** Teach me Your way, O Lord, and lead me in a smooth path, because of my enemies.

### Psalm 31:3

**KJV:** For thou art my rock and my fortress; therefore for thy name's sake lead me, and guide me.

**NKJV:** For You are my rock and my fortress; therefore, for Your name's sake, lead me and guide me.

### Psalm 32:8–9

**KJV:** I will instruct thee and teach thee in the way which thou shalt go: I will guide thee with mine eye. Be ye not as the horse, or as the mule, which have no understanding: whose mouth must be held in with bit and bridle, lest they come near unto thee.

**NKJV:** I will instruct you and teach you in the way you should go; I will guide you with My eye. Do not be like the horse or like the mule, which have no understanding, which must be harnessed with bit and bridle, else they will not come near you.

### Psalm 37:5

**KJV:** Commit thy way unto the Lord; trust also in him; and he shall bring it to pass.

**NKJV:** Commit your way to the Lord, trust also in Him, and He shall bring it to pass.

### Psalm 37:23

**KJV:** The steps of a good man are ordered by the Lord: and he delighteth in his way.

**NKJV:** The steps of a good man are ordered by the Lord, and He delights in his way.

### Psalm 61:1–2

**KJV:** Hear my cry, O God; attend unto my prayer. From the end of the earth will I cry unto thee, when my heart is overwhelmed: lead me to the rock that is higher than I.

**NKJV:** Hear my cry, O God; attend to my prayer. From the end of the earth I will cry to You, when my heart is overwhelmed; lead me to the rock that is higher than I.

### Psalm 73:23–24

**KJV:** Nevertheless I am continually with thee: thou hast holden me by my right hand. Thou shalt guide me with thy counsel, and afterward receive me to glory.

**NKJV:** Nevertheless I am continually with You; You hold me by my right hand. You will guide me with Your counsel, and afterward receive me to glory.

### Proverbs 3:5–6

**KJV:** Trust in the Lord with all thine heart; and lean not unto thine own understanding. In all thy ways acknowledge him, and he shall direct thy paths.

**NKJV:** Trust in the Lord with all your heart, and lean not on your own understanding; in all your ways acknowledge Him, and He shall direct your paths.

### Proverbs 16:3

**KJV:** Commit thy works unto the Lord, and thy thoughts shall be established.

**NKJV:** Commit your works to the Lord, and your thoughts will be established.

### John 10:3–5

**KJV:** To him the porter openeth; and the sheep hear his voice: and he calleth his own sheep by name, and leadeth them out. And when he putteth forth his own sheep, he goeth before them, and the sheep follow him: for they know his voice. And a stranger will they not follow, but will flee from him: for they know not the voice of strangers.

**NKJV:** To him the doorkeeper opens, and the sheep hear his voice; and he calls his own sheep by name and leads them out. And when he brings out his own sheep, he goes before them; and the sheep follow him, for they know his voice. Yet they will by no means follow a stranger, but will flee from him, for they do not know the voice of strangers.

### John 16:13–15

**KJV:** Howbeit when he, the Spirit of truth, is come, he will guide you into all truth: for he shall not speak of himself; but whatsoever he shall hear, that shall he speak: and he will shew you things to come. He shall glorify me: for he shall receive of mine, and shall shew it unto you. All things that the Father hath are mine: therefore said I, that he shall take of mine, and shall shew it unto you.

**NKJV:** However, when He, the Spirit of truth, has come, He will guide you into all truth; for He will not speak on His own authority, but whatever He hears He will speak; and He will tell you things to come. He will glorify Me, for He will take of what is Mine and declare it to you. All things that the Father has are Mine. Therefore I said that He will take of Mine and declare it to you.

### Romans 8:14

**KJV:** For as many as are led by the Spirit of God, they are the sons of God.

**NKJV:** For as many as are led by the Spirit of God, these are sons of God.

### Romans 12:1–2

**KJV:** I beseech you therefore, brethren, by the mercies of God, that ye present your bodies a living sacrifice, holy, acceptable unto God, which is your reasonable service. And be not conformed to this world: but be ye transformed by the renewing of your mind, that ye may prove what is that good, and acceptable, and perfect, will of God.

**NKJV:** I beseech you therefore, brethren, by the mercies of God, that you present your bodies a living sacrifice, holy, acceptable to God, which is your reasonable service. And do not be conformed to this world, but be transformed by the renewing of your mind, that you may prove what is that good and acceptable and perfect will of God.

### Colossians 1:9–10

**KJV:** For this cause we also, since the day we heard it, do not cease to pray for you, and to desire that ye might be filled with the knowledge of his will in all wisdom and spiritual understanding; that ye might walk worthy of the Lord unto all pleasing, being fruitful in every good work, and increasing in the knowledge of God.

**NKJV:** For this reason we also, since the day we heard it, do not cease to pray for you, and to ask that you may be filled with the knowledge of His will in all wisdom and spiritual understanding; that you may walk worthy of the Lord, fully pleasing Him, being fruitful in every good work and increasing in the knowledge of God.

### James 1:5

**KJV:** If any of you lack wisdom, let him ask of God, that giveth to all men liberally, and upbraideth not; and it shall be given him.

**NKJV:** If any of you lacks wisdom, let him ask of God, who gives to all liberally and without reproach, and it will be given to him.

Pray the Word

# 15

# Discipline Diligence

"Thank You, Father, that today I have the plans of the diligent."
Proverbs 21:5

### Proverbs 6:6–11

**KJV:** Go to the ant, thou sluggard; consider her ways, and be wise: which having no guide, overseer, or ruler, provideth her meat in the summer, and gathereth her food in the harvest. How long wilt thou sleep, O sluggard? When wilt thou arise out of thy sleep? Yet a little sleep, a little slumber, a little folding of the hands to sleep: so shall thy poverty come as one that travelleth, and thy want as an armed man.

**NKJV:** Go to the ant, you sluggard! Consider her ways and be wise, which, having no captain, overseer or ruler, provides her supplies in the summer, and gathers her food in the harvest. How long will you slumber, O sluggard? When will you rise from your sleep? A little sleep, a little slumber, a little folding of the hands to sleep—so shall your poverty come on you like a prowler, and your need like an armed man.

### Proverbs 10:4

**KJV:** He becometh poor that dealeth with a slack hand: but the hand of the diligent maketh rich.

**NKJV:** He who has a slack hand becomes poor, but the hand of the diligent makes rich.

### Proverbs 12:24

**KJV:** The hand of the diligent shall bear rule: but the slothful shall be under tribute.

**NKJV:** The hand of the diligent will rule, but the lazy man will be put to forced labor.

### Proverbs 15:19

**KJV:** The way of the slothful man is as an hedge of thorns: but the way of the righteous is made plain.

**NKJV:** The way of the lazy man is like a hedge of thorns, but the way of the upright is a highway.

### Proverbs 21:5

**KJV:** The thoughts of the diligent tend only to plenteousness; but of every one that is hasty only to want.

**NKJV:** The plans of the diligent lead surely to plenty, but those of everyone who is hasty, surely to poverty.

*Discipline | Diligence*

### Daniel 1:8

**KJV:** But Daniel purposed in his heart that he would not defile himself with the portion of the king's meat, nor with the wine which he drank: therefore he requested of the prince of the eunuchs that he might not defile himself.

**NKJV:** But Daniel purposed in his heart that he would not defile himself with the portion of the king's delicacies, nor with the wine which he drank; therefore he requested of the chief of the eunuchs that he might not defile himself.

### Matthew 7:13–14

**KJV:** Enter ye in at the strait gate: for wide is the gate, and broad is the way, that leadeth to destruction, and many there be which go in thereat: because strait is the gate, and narrow is the way, which leadeth unto life, and few there be that find it.

**NKJV:** Enter by the narrow gate; for wide is the gate and broad is the way that leads to destruction, and there are many who go in by it. Because narrow is the gate and difficult is the way which leads to life, and there are few who find it.

### John 8:31–32

**KJV:** Then said Jesus to those Jews which believed on him, If ye continue in my word, then are ye my disciples indeed; and ye shall know the truth, and the truth shall make you free.

**NKJV:** Then Jesus said to those Jews who believed Him, "If you abide in My word, you are My disciples indeed. And you shall know the truth, and the truth shall make you free."

### Romans 13:14

**KJV:** But put ye on the Lord Jesus Christ, and make not provision for the flesh, to fulfil the lusts thereof.

**NKJV:** But put on the Lord Jesus Christ, and make no provision for the flesh, to fulfill its lusts.

### 1 Corinthians 9:24–27

**KJV:** Know ye not that they which run in a race run all, but one receiveth the prize? So run, that ye may obtain. And every man that striveth for the mastery is temperate in all things. Now they do it to obtain a corruptible crown; but we an incorruptible. I therefore so run, not as uncertainly; so fight I, not as one that beateth the air: but I keep under my body, and bring it into subjection: lest that by any means, when I have preached to others, I myself should be a castaway.

**NKJV:** Do you not know that those who run in a race all run, but one receives the prize? Run in such a way that you may obtain it. And everyone who competes for the prize is temperate in all things. Now they do it to obtain a perishable crown, but we for an imperishable crown. Therefore I run thus: not with uncertainty. Thus I fight: not as one who beats the air. But I discipline my body and bring it into subjection, lest, when I have preached to others, I myself should become disqualified.

### 1 Timothy 4:8

**KJV:** For bodily exercise profiteth little: but godliness is profitable unto all things, having promise of the life that now is, and of that which is to come.

**NKJV:** For bodily exercise profits a little, but godliness is profitable for all things, having promise of the life that now is and of that which is to come.

### Hebrews 12:1

**KJV:** Wherefore seeing we also are compassed about with so great a cloud of witnesses, let us lay aside every weight, and the sin which doth so easily beset us, and let us run with patience the race that is set before us.

**NKJV:** Therefore we also, since we are surrounded by so great a cloud of witnesses, let us lay aside every weight, and the sin which so easily ensnares us, and let us run with endurance the race that is set before us.

# Pray the Word

# 16 Evangelism

> "Thank You, Father, that today I am bold and unashamed of the gospel of Jesus."
> Romans 1:16

### Psalm 105:1

**KJV:** O give thanks unto the Lord; call upon his name: make known his deeds among the people.

**NKJV:** Oh, give thanks to the Lord! Call upon His name; make known His deeds among the peoples!

### Proverbs 11:30

**KJV:** The fruit of the righteous is a tree of life; and he that winneth souls is wise.

**NKJV:** The fruit of the righteous is a tree of life, and he who wins souls is wise.

### Isaiah 6:8

**KJV:** Also I heard the voice of the Lord, saying, Whom shall I send, and who will go for us? Then said I, Here am I; send me.

**NKJV:** Also I heard the voice of the Lord, saying: "Whom shall I send, and who will go for Us?" Then I said, "Here am I! Send me."

### Isaiah 12:4

**KJV:** And in that day shall ye say, Praise the Lord, call upon his name, declare his doings among the people, make mention that his name is exalted.

**NKJV:** And in that day you will say: "Praise the Lord, call upon His name; declare His deeds among the peoples, make mention that His name is exalted."

### Isaiah 45:22

**KJV:** Look unto me, and be ye saved, all the ends of the earth: for I am God, and there is none else.

**NKJV:** Look to Me, and be saved, all you ends of the earth! For I am God, and there is no other.

### Matthew 5:15–16

**KJV:** Neither do men light a candle, and put it under a bushel, but on a candlestick; and it giveth light unto all that are in the house. Let your light so shine before men, that they may see your good works, and glorify your Father which is in heaven.

**NKJV:** Nor do they light a lamp and put it under a basket, but on a lampstand, and it gives light to all who are in the house. Let your light so shine before men, that they may see your good works and glorify your Father in heaven.

## Evangelism

### Matthew 9:37–38

**KJV:** Then saith he unto his disciples, The harvest truly is plenteous, but the labourers are few; pray ye therefore the Lord of the harvest, that he will send forth labourers into his harvest.

**NKJV:** Then He said to His disciples, "The harvest truly is plentiful, but the laborers are few. Therefore pray the Lord of the harvest to send out laborers into His harvest."

### Matthew 28:19–20

**KJV:** Go ye therefore, and teach all nations, baptizing them in the name of the Father, and of the Son, and of the Holy Ghost: teaching them to observe all things whatsoever I have commanded you: and, lo, I am with you always, even unto the end of the world. Amen.

**NKJV:** "Go therefore and make disciples of all the nations, baptizing them in the name of the Father and of the Son and of the Holy Spirit, teaching them to observe all things that I have commanded you; and lo, I am with you always, even to the end of the age." Amen.

### Mark 16:15

**KJV:** And he said unto them, Go ye into all the world, and preach the gospel to every creature.

**NKJV:** And He said to them, "Go into all the world and preach the gospel to every creature."

### Luke 12:8

**KJV:** Also I say unto you, whosoever shall confess me before men, him shall the Son of man also confess before the angels of God.

**NKJV:** Also I say to you, whoever confesses Me before men, him the Son of Man also will confess before the angels of God.

### John 3:16–17

**KJV:** For God so loved the world, that he gave his only begotten Son, that whosoever believeth in him should not perish, but have everlasting life. For God sent not his Son into the world to condemn the world; but that the world through him might be saved.

**NKJV:** For God so loved the world that He gave His only begotten Son, that whoever believes in Him should not perish but have everlasting life. For God did not send His Son into the world to condemn the world, but that the world through Him might be saved.

### John 4:35b

**KJV:** Behold, I say unto you, lift up your eyes, and look on the fields; for they are white already to harvest.

**NKJV:** Behold, I say to you, lift up your eyes and look at the fields, for they are already white for harvest!

### John 14:6

**KJV:** Jesus saith unto him, I am the way, the truth, and the life: no man cometh unto the Father, but by me.

**NKJV:** Jesus said to him, "I am the way, the truth, and the life. No one comes to the Father except through Me."

### John 15:8

**KJV:** Herein is my Father glorified, that ye bear much fruit; so shall ye be my disciples.

**NKJV:** By this My Father is glorified, that you bear much fruit; so you will be My disciples.

### John 15:16

**KJV:** Ye have not chosen me, but I have chosen you, and ordained you, that ye should go and bring forth fruit, and that your fruit should remain: that whatsoever ye shall ask of the Father in my name, he may give it you.

**NKJV:** You did not choose Me, but I chose you and appointed you that you should go and bear fruit, and that your fruit should remain, that whatever you ask the Father in My name He may give you.

### Acts 1:8

**KJV:** But ye shall receive power, after that the Holy Ghost is come upon you: and ye shall be witnesses unto me both in Jerusalem, and in all Judaea, and in Samaria, and unto the uttermost part of the earth.

**NKJV:** But you shall receive power when the Holy Spirit has come upon you; and you shall be witnesses to Me in Jerusalem, and in all Judea and Samaria, and to the end of the earth.

### Acts 20:24

**KJV:** But none of these things move me, neither count I my life dear unto myself, so that I might finish my course with joy, and the ministry, which I have received of the Lord Jesus, to testify the gospel of the grace of God.

**NKJV:** But none of these things move me; nor do I count my life dear to myself, so that I may finish my race with joy, and the ministry which I received from the Lord Jesus, to testify to the gospel of the grace of God.

### Romans 1:16

**KJV:** For I am not ashamed of the gospel of Christ: for it is the power of God unto salvation to every one that believeth; to the Jew first, and also to the Greek.

**NKJV:** For I am not ashamed of the gospel of Christ, for it is the power of God to salvation for everyone who believes, for the Jew first and also for the Greek.

### Romans 10:10–17

**KJV:** For with the heart man believeth unto righteousness; and with the mouth confession is made unto salvation. For the scripture saith, Whosoever believeth on him shall not be ashamed. For there is no difference between the Jew and the Greek: for the same Lord over all is rich unto all that call upon him. For whosoever shall call upon the name of the Lord shall be saved. How then shall they call on him in whom they have not believed? And how shall they believe in him of whom they have not heard? And how shall they hear without a preacher? And how shall they preach, except they be sent? As it is written, How beautiful are the feet of them that preach the gospel of peace, and bring glad tidings of good things! But they have not all obeyed the gospel. For Esaias saith, Lord, who hath believed our report? So then faith cometh by hearing, and hearing by the word of God.

**NKJV:** For with the heart one believes unto righteousness, and with the mouth confession is made unto salvation. For the Scripture says, "Whoever believes on Him will not be put to shame." For there is no distinction between Jew and Greek, for the same Lord over all is rich to all who call upon Him. For "whoever calls on the name of the Lord shall be saved." How then shall they call on Him in whom they have not believed? And how shall they believe in Him of whom they have not heard? And how shall they hear without a preacher? And how shall they preach unless they are sent? As it is written: "How beautiful are the feet of those who preach the gospel of peace, who bring glad tidings of good things!" But they have not all obeyed the gospel. For Isaiah says, "Lord, who has believed our report?" So then faith comes by hearing, and hearing by the word of God.

## Evangelism

### 1 Corinthians 2:1–2

**KJV:** And I, brethren, when I came to you, came not with excellency of speech or of wisdom, declaring unto you the testimony of God. For I determined not to know any thing among you, save Jesus Christ, and him crucified.

**NKJV:** And I, brethren, when I came to you, did not come with excellence of speech or of wisdom declaring to you the testimony of God. For I determined not to know anything among you except Jesus Christ and Him crucified.

### 1 Corinthians 3:6–9

**KJV:** I have planted, Apollos watered; but God gave the increase. So then neither is he that planteth any thing, neither he that watereth; but God that giveth the increase. Now he that planteth and he that watereth are one: and every man shall receive his own reward according to his own labour. for we are labourers together with God: ye are God's husbandry, ye are God's building.

**NKJV:** I planted, Apollos watered, but God gave the increase. So then neither he who plants is anything, nor he who waters, but God who gives the increase. Now he who plants and he who waters are one, and each one will receive his own reward according to his own labor. For we are God's fellow workers; you are God's field, you are God's building.

### 1 Corinthians 9:19–23

**KJV:** For though I be free from all men, yet have I made myself servant unto all, that I might gain the more. And unto the Jews I became as a Jew, that I might gain the Jews; to them that are under the law, as under the law, that I might gain them that are under the law; to them that are without law, as without law, (being not without law to God, but under the law to Christ,) that I might gain them that are without law. To the weak became I as weak, that I might gain the weak: I am made all things to all men, that I might by all means save some. And this I do for the gospel's sake, that I might be partaker thereof with you.

**NKJV:** For though I am free from all men, I have made myself a servant to all, that I might win the more; and to the Jews I became as a Jew, that I might win Jews; to those who are under the law, as under the law, that I might win those who are under the law; to those who are without law, as without law (not being without law toward God, but under law toward Christ), that I might win those who are without law; to the weak I became as weak, that I might win the weak. I have become all things to all men, that I might by all means save some. Now this I do for the gospel's sake, that I may be partaker of it with you.

### 1 Corinthians 16:7–9

**KJV:** For I will not see you now by the way; but I trust to tarry a while with you, if the Lord permit. But I will tarry at Ephesus until Pentecost. For a great door and effectual is opened unto me, and there are many adversaries.

**NKJV:** For I do not wish to see you now on the way; but I hope to stay a while with you, if the Lord permits. But I will tarry in Ephesus until Pentecost. For a great and effective door has opened to me, and there are many adversaries.

### 2 Corinthians 5:20

**KJV:** Now then we are ambassadors for Christ, as though God did beseech you by us: we pray you in Christ's stead, be ye reconciled to God.

**NKJV:** Now then, we are ambassadors for Christ, as though God were pleading through us: we implore you on Christ's behalf, be reconciled to God.

### Colossians 4:2–6

**KJV:** Continue in prayer, and watch in the same with thanksgiving; withal praying also for us, that God would open unto us a door of utterance, to speak the mystery of Christ, for which I am also in bonds: that I may make it manifest, as I ought to speak. Walk in wisdom toward them that are without, redeeming the time. Let your speech be alway with grace, seasoned with salt, that ye may know how ye ought to answer every man.

**NKJV:** Continue earnestly in prayer, being vigilant in it with thanksgiving; meanwhile praying also for us, that God would open to us a door for the word, to speak the mystery of Christ, for which I am also in chains, that I may make it manifest, as I ought to speak. Walk in wisdom toward those who are outside, redeeming the time. Let your speech always be with grace, seasoned with salt, that you may know how you ought to answer each one.

### 1 Thessalonians 1:5

**KJV:** For our gospel came not unto you in word only, but also in power, and in the Holy Ghost, and in much assurance; as ye know what manner of men we were among you for your sake.

**NKJV:** For our gospel did not come to you in word only, but also in power, and in the Holy Spirit and in much assurance, as you know what kind of men we were among you for your sake.

### 2 Timothy 4:5

**KJV:** But watch thou in all things, endure afflictions, do the work of an evangelist, make full proof of thy ministry.

**NKJV:** But you be watchful in all things, endure afflictions, do the work of an evangelist, fulfill your ministry.

### 1 Peter 3:15

**KJV:** But sanctify the Lord God in your hearts: and be ready always to give an answer to every man that asketh you a reason of the hope that is in you with meekness and fear.

**NKJV:** But sanctify the Lord God in your hearts, and always be ready to give a defense to everyone who asks you a reason for the hope that is in you, with meekness and fear.

### 2 Peter 3:9

**KJV:** The Lord is not slack concerning his promise, as some men count slackness; but is longsuffering to us-ward, not willing that any should perish, but that all should come to repentance.

**NKJV:** The Lord is not slack concerning His promise, as some count slackness, but is longsuffering toward us, not willing that any should perish but that all should come to repentance.

# 17 Faith

> "Thank You, Father, that I walk by faith and not by sight."
> 2 Corinthians 5:7

### Matthew 15:28

**KJV:** Then Jesus answered and said unto her, O woman, great is thy faith: be it unto thee even as thou wilt. And her daughter was made whole from that very hour.

**NKJV:** Then Jesus answered and said to her, "O woman, great is your faith! Let it be to you as you desire." And her daughter was healed from that very hour.

### Matthew 17:20

**KJV:** And Jesus said unto them, Because of your unbelief: for verily I say unto you, if ye have faith as a grain of mustard seed, ye shall say unto this mountain, Remove hence to yonder place; and it shall remove; and nothing shall be impossible unto you.

**NKJV:** So Jesus said to them, "Because of your unbelief; for assuredly, I say to you, if you have faith as a mustard seed, you will say to this mountain, 'Move from here to there,' and it will move; and nothing will be impossible for you."

### Matthew 21:21

**KJV:** Jesus answered and said unto them, Verily I say unto you, if ye have faith, and doubt not, ye shall not only do this which is done to the fig tree, but also if ye shall say unto this mountain, Be thou removed, and be thou cast into the sea; it shall be done.

**NKJV:** So Jesus answered and said to them, "Assuredly, I say to you, if you have faith and do not doubt, you will not only do what was done to the fig tree, but also if you say to this mountain, 'Be removed and be cast into the sea,' it will be done."

### Mark 10:52

**KJV:** And Jesus said unto him, Go thy way; thy faith hath made thee whole. And immediately he received his sight, and followed Jesus in the way.

**NKJV:** Then Jesus said to him, "Go your way; your faith has made you well." And immediately he received his sight and followed Jesus on the road.

### Mark 11:23–24

**KJV:** For verily I say unto you, that whosoever shall say unto this mountain, Be thou removed, and be thou cast into the sea; and shall not doubt in his heart, but shall believe that those things which he saith shall come to pass; he shall have whatsoever he saith. Therefore I say unto you, What things soever ye desire, when ye pray, believe that ye receive them, and ye shall have them.

**NKJV:** For assuredly, I say to you, whoever says to this mountain, "Be removed and be cast into the sea," and does not doubt in his heart, but believes that those things he says will be done, he will have whatever he says. Therefore I say to you, whatever things you ask when you pray, believe that you receive them, and you will have them.

### Luke 17:6

**KJV:** And the Lord said, If ye had faith as a grain of mustard seed, ye might say unto this sycamine tree, Be thou plucked up by the root, and be thou planted in the sea; and it should obey you.

**NKJV:** So the Lord said, "If you have faith as a mustard seed, you can say to this mulberry tree, 'Be pulled up by the roots and be planted in the sea,' and it would obey you."

### John 11:40

**KJV:** Jesus saith unto her, Said I not unto thee, that, if thou wouldest believe, thou shouldest see the glory of God?

**NKJV:** Jesus said to her, "Did I not say to you that if you would believe you would see the glory of God?"

### Romans 1:17

**KJV:** For therein is the righteousness of God revealed from faith to faith: as it is written, The just shall live by faith.

**NKJV:** For in it the righteousness of God is revealed from faith to faith; as it is written, "The just shall live by faith."

### Romans 4:16

**KJV:** Therefore it is of faith, that it might be by grace; to the end the promise might be sure to all the seed; not to that only which is of the law, but to that also which is of the faith of Abraham; who is the father of us all.

**NKJV:** Therefore it is of faith that it might be according to grace, so that the promise might be sure to all the seed, not only to those who are of the law, but also to those who are of the faith of Abraham, who is the father of us all.

### Romans 10:17

**KJV:** So then faith cometh by hearing, and hearing by the word of God.

**NKJV:** So then faith comes by hearing, and hearing by the word of God.

### 1 Corinthians 2:5

**KJV:** That your faith should not stand in the wisdom of men, but in the power of God.

**NKJV:** That your faith should not be in the wisdom of men but in the power of God.

### 1 Corinthians 16:13

**KJV:** Watch ye, stand fast in the faith, quit you like men, be strong.

**NKJV:** Watch, stand fast in the faith, be brave, be strong.

### 2 Corinthians 1:24

**KJV:** Not for that we have dominion over your faith, but are helpers of your joy: for by faith ye stand.

**NKJV:** Not that we have dominion over your faith, but are fellow workers for your joy; for by faith you stand.

### 2 Corinthians 5:7

**KJV:** For we walk by faith, not by sight.

**NKJV:** For we walk by faith, not by sight.

### Galatians 2:20

**KJV:** I am crucified with Christ: nevertheless I live; yet not I, but Christ liveth in me: and the life which I now live in the flesh I live by the faith of the Son of God, who loved me, and gave himself for me.

**NKJV:** I have been crucified with Christ; it is no longer I who live, but Christ lives in me; and the life which I now live in the flesh I live by faith in the Son of God, who loved me and gave Himself for me.

### Ephesians 6:16

**KJV:** Above all, taking the shield of faith, wherewith ye shall be able to quench all the fiery darts of the wicked.

**NKJV:** Above all, taking the shield of faith with which you will be able to quench all the fiery darts of the wicked one.

### 1 Timothy 6:11

**KJV:** But thou, O man of God, flee these things; and follow after righteousness, godliness, faith, love, patience, meekness.

**NKJV:** But you, O man of God, flee these things and pursue righteousness, godliness, faith, love, patience, gentleness.

### 1 Timothy 6:12

**KJV:** Fight the good fight of faith, lay hold on eternal life, whereunto thou art also called, and hast professed a good profession before many witnesses.

**NKJV:** Fight the good fight of faith, lay hold on eternal life, to which you were also called and have confessed the good confession in the presence of many witnesses.

### 2 Timothy 4:7

**KJV:** I have fought a good fight, I have finished my course, I have kept the faith.

**NKJV:** I have fought the good fight, I have finished the race, I have kept the faith.

### Hebrews 4:3

**KJV:** For we which have believed do enter into rest, as he said, As I have sworn in my wrath, if they shall enter into my rest: although the works were finished from the foundation of the world.

**NKJV:** For we who have believed do enter that rest, as He has said: "So I swore in My wrath, 'They shall not enter My rest,'" although the works were finished from the foundation of the world.

### Hebrews 11:1

**KJV:** Now faith is the substance of things hoped for, the evidence of things not seen.

**NKJV:** Now faith is the substance of things hoped for, the evidence of things not seen.

### Hebrews 11:6

**KJV:** But without faith it is impossible to please him: for he that cometh to God must believe that he is, and that he is a rewarder of them that diligently seek him.

**NKJV:** But without faith it is impossible to please Him, for he who comes to God must believe that He is, and that He is a rewarder of those who diligently seek Him.

### Hebrews 11:7

**KJV:** By faith Noah, being warned of God of things not seen as yet, moved with fear, prepared an ark to the saving of his house; by the which he condemned the world, and became heir of the righteousness which is by faith.

**NKJV:** By faith Noah, being divinely warned of things not yet seen, moved with godly fear, prepared an ark for the saving of his household, by which he condemned the world and became heir of the righteousness which is according to faith.

### Hebrews 11:11

**KJV:** Through faith also Sara herself received strength to conceive seed, and was delivered of a child when she was past age, because she judged him faithful who had promised.

**NKJV:** By faith Sarah herself also received strength to conceive seed, and she bore a child when she was past the age, because she judged Him faithful who had promised.

### Hebrews 12:1

**KJV:** Wherefore seeing we also are compassed about with so great a cloud of witnesses, let us lay aside every weight, and the sin which doth so easily beset us, and let us run with patience the race that is set before us.

**NKJV:** Therefore we also, since we are surrounded by so great a cloud of witnesses, let us lay aside every weight, and the sin which so easily ensnares us, and let us run with endurance the race that is set before us.

### James 1:6

**KJV:** But let him ask in faith, nothing wavering. For he that wavereth is like a wave of the sea driven with the wind and tossed.

**NKJV:** But let him ask in faith, with no doubting, for he who doubts is like a wave of the sea driven and tossed by the wind.

### 1 Peter 5:8–9

**KJV:** Be sober, be vigilant; because your adversary the devil, as a roaring lion, walketh about, seeking whom he may devour: whom resist stedfast in the faith, knowing that the same afflictions are accomplished in your brethren that are in the world.

**NKJV:** Be sober, be vigilant; because your adversary the devil walks about like a roaring lion, seeking whom he may devour. Resist him, steadfast in the faith, knowing that the same sufferings are experienced by your brotherhood in the world.

### 1 John 5:4

**KJV:** For whatsoever is born of God overcometh the world: and this is the victory that overcometh the world, even our faith.

**NKJV:** For whatever is born of God overcomes the world. And this is the victory that has overcome the world—our faith.

# 18 Faithfulness

> "Thank You, Father, that I am steadfast,
> immovable, always abounding
> in the work of the Lord."
> 1 Corinthians 15:58

### Proverbs 20:6

**KJV:** Most men will proclaim every one his own goodness: but a faithful man who can find?

**NKJV:** Most men will proclaim each his own goodness, but who can find a faithful man?

### Proverbs 28:20

**KJV:** A faithful man shall abound with blessings: but he that maketh haste to be rich shall not be innocent.

**NKJV:** A faithful man will abound with blessings, but he who hastens to be rich will not go unpunished.

### Matthew 25:21

**KJV:** His Lord said unto him, Well done, thou good and faithful servant: thou hast been faithful over a few things, I will make thee ruler over many things: enter thou into the joy of thy Lord.

**NKJV:** His Lord said to him, "Well done, good and faithful servant; you were faithful over a few things, I will make you ruler over many things. Enter into the joy of your Lord."

### Luke 12:42–44

**KJV:** And the Lord said, Who then is that faithful and wise steward, whom his Lord shall make ruler over his household, to give them their portion of meat in due season? Blessed is that servant, whom his Lord when he cometh shall find so doing. Of a truth I say unto you, that he will make him ruler over all that he hath.

**NKJV:** And the Lord said, "Who then is that faithful and wise steward, whom his master will make ruler over his household, to give them their portion of food in due season? Blessed is that servant whom his master will find so doing when he comes. Truly, I say to you that he will make him ruler over all that he has."

### Luke 16:10–12

**KJV:** He that is faithful in that which is least is faithful also in much: and he that is unjust in the least is unjust also in much. If therefore ye have not been faithful in the unrighteous mammon, who will commit to your trust the true riches? And if ye have not been faithful in that which is another man's, who shall give you that which is your own?

**NKJV:** He who is faithful in what is least is faithful also in much; and he who is unjust in what is least is unjust also in much. Therefore if you have not been faithful in the unrighteous mammon, who will commit to your trust the true riches? And if you have not been faithful in what is another man's, who will give you what is your own?

### 1 Corinthians 4:2

**KJV:** Moreover it is required in stewards, that a man be found faithful.

**NKJV:** Moreover it is required in stewards that one be found faithful.

### 1 Corinthians 15:58

**KJV:** Therefore, my beloved brethren, be ye stedfast, unmoveable, always abounding in the work of the Lord, forasmuch as ye know that your labour is not in vain in the Lord.

**NKJV:** Therefore, my beloved brethren, be steadfast, immovable, always abounding in the work of the Lord, knowing that your labor is not in vain in the Lord.

### 1 Corinthians 16:13

**KJV:** Watch ye, stand fast in the faith, quit you like men, be strong.

**NKJV:** Watch, stand fast in the faith, be brave, be strong.

### 2 Timothy 1:12

**KJV:** For the which cause I also suffer these things: nevertheless I am not ashamed: for I know whom I have believed, and am persuaded that he is able to keep that which I have committed unto him against that day.

**NKJV:** For this reason I also suffer these things; nevertheless I am not ashamed, for I know whom I have believed and am persuaded that He is able to keep what I have committed to Him until that Day.

### 2 Timothy 2:2

**KJV:** And the things that thou hast heard of me among many witnesses, the same commit thou to faithful men, who shall be able to teach others also.

**NKJV:** And the things that you have heard from me among many witnesses, commit these to faithful men who will be able to teach others also.

### 2 Timothy 4:7

**KJV:** I have fought a good fight, I have finished my course, I have kept the faith.

**NKJV:** I have fought the good fight, I have finished the race, I have kept the faith.

### Revelation 17:14

**KJV:** These shall make war with the Lamb, and the Lamb shall overcome them: for he is Lord of lords, and King of kings: and they that are with him are called, and chosen, and faithful.

**NKJV:** These will make war with the Lamb, and the Lamb will overcome them, for He is Lord of lords and King of kings; and those who are with Him are called, chosen, and faithful.

# 19 Favor

> "Thank You, Father, that I am encompassed about as a shield with Your favor."
> Psalm 5:12

### Psalm 5:12

**KJV:** For thou, Lord, wilt bless the righteous; with favour wilt thou compass him as with a shield.

**NKJV:** For You, O Lord, will bless the righteous; with favor You will surround him as with a shield.

### Psalm 75:6–7

**KJV:** For promotion cometh neither from the east, nor from the west, nor from the south. But God is the judge: he putteth down one, and setteth up another.

**NKJV:** For exaltation comes neither from the east nor from the west nor from the south. But God is the Judge: He puts down one, and exalts another.

### Psalm 89:17

**KJV:** For thou art the glory of their strength: and in thy favour our horn shall be exalted.

**NKJV:** For You are the glory of their strength, and in Your favor our horn is exalted.

### Psalm 92:10

**KJV:** But my horn shalt thou exalt like the horn of an unicorn: I shall be anointed with fresh oil.

**NKJV:** But my horn You have exalted like a wild ox; I have been anointed with fresh oil.

### Proverbs 3:3–4

**KJV:** Let not mercy and truth forsake thee: bind them about thy neck; write them upon the table of thine heart: so shalt thou find favour and good understanding in the sight of God and man.

**NKJV:** Let not mercy and truth forsake you; bind them around your neck, write them on the tablet of your heart, and so find favor and high esteem in the sight of God and man.

### Proverbs 12:2

**KJV:** A good man obtaineth favour of the Lord: but a man of wicked devices will he condemn.

**NKJV:** A good man obtains favor from the Lord, but a man of wicked intentions He will condemn.

### Proverbs 13:15

**KJV:** Good understanding giveth favour: but the way of transgressors is hard.

**NKJV:** Good understanding gains favor, but the way of the unfaithful is hard.

### Luke 2:52

**KJV:** And Jesus increased in wisdom and stature, and in favour with God and man.

**NKJV:** And Jesus increased in wisdom and stature, and in favor with God and men.

Pray the Word

# 20

## Fear Courage

> "Thank You, Father, that You have not given me a spirit of fear but of power, love, and a sound mind."
> 2 Timothy 1:7

### Joshua 1:7–9

**KJV:** Only be thou strong and very courageous, that thou mayest observe to do according to all the law, which Moses my servant commanded thee: turn not from it to the right hand or to the left, that thou mayest prosper whithersoever thou goest. This book of the law shall not depart out of thy mouth; but thou shalt meditate therein day and night, that thou mayest observe to do according to all that is written therein: for then thou shalt make thy way prosperous, and then thou shalt have good success. Have not I commanded thee? Be strong and of a good courage; be not afraid, neither be thou dismayed: for the Lord thy God is with thee whithersoever thou goest.

**NKJV:** Only be strong and very courageous, that you may observe to do according to all the law which Moses My servant commanded you; do not turn from it to the right hand or to the left, that you may prosper wherever you go. This Book of the Law shall not depart from your mouth, but you shall meditate in it day and night, that you may observe to do according to all that is written in it. For then you will make your way prosperous, and then you will have good success. Have I not commanded you? Be strong and of good courage; do not be afraid, nor be dismayed, for the Lord your God is with you wherever you go.

### Psalm 23:4

**KJV:** Yea, though I walk through the valley of the shadow of death, I will fear no evil: for thou art with me; thy rod and thy staff they comfort me.

**NKJV:** Yea, though I walk through the valley of the shadow of death, I will fear no evil; for You are with me; Your rod and Your staff, they comfort me.

### Psalm 27:14

**KJV:** Wait on the Lord: be of good courage, and he shall strengthen thine heart: wait, I say, on the Lord.

**NKJV:** Wait on the Lord; be of good courage, and He shall strengthen your heart; wait, I say, on the Lord!

### Psalm 112:7–8

**KJV:** He shall not be afraid of evil tidings: his heart is fixed, trusting in the Lord. His heart is established, he shall not be afraid, until he see his desire upon his enemies.

**NKJV:** He will not be afraid of evil tidings; His heart is steadfast, trusting in the Lord. His heart is established; He will not be afraid, Until he sees his desire upon his enemies.

Fear | Courage

### Psalm 112:7–8

**KJV:** The LORD is on my side; I will not fear: what can man do unto me?

**NKJV:** The LORD is on my side; I will not fear. What can man do to me?

### Proverbs 1:33

**KJV:** But whoso hearkeneth unto me shall dwell safely, and shall be quiet from fear of evil.

**NKJV:** But whoever listens to me will dwell safely, and will be secure, without fear of evil.

### Isaiah 41:10

**KJV:** Fear thou not; for I am with thee: be not dismayed; for I am thy God: I will strengthen thee; yea, I will help thee; yea, I will uphold thee with the right hand of my righteousness.

**NKJV:** Fear not, for I am with you; be not dismayed, for I am your God. I will strengthen you, yes, I will help you, I will uphold you with My righteous right hand.

### Isaiah 43:1–2

**KJV:** But now thus saith the LORD that created thee, O Jacob, and he that formed thee, O Israel, fear not: for I have redeemed thee, I have called thee by thy name; thou art mine. When thou passest through the waters, I will be with thee; and through the rivers, they shall not overflow thee: when thou walkest through the fire, thou shalt not be burned; neither shall the flame kindle upon thee.

**NKJV:** But now, thus says the LORD, who created you, O Jacob, And He who formed you, O Israel: "Fear not, for I have redeemed you; I have called you by your name; You are Mine. When you pass through the waters, I will be with you; and through the rivers, they shall not overflow you. When you walk through the fire, you shall not be burned, nor shall the flame scorch you."

### Jeremiah 1:7

**KJV:** But the Lord said unto me, Say not, I am a child: for thou shalt go to all that I shall send thee, and whatsoever I command thee thou shalt speak.

**NKJV:** But the Lord said to me: "Do not say, 'I am a youth,' For you shall go to all to whom I send you, and whatever I command you, you shall speak."

### Mark 5:36

**KJV:** As soon as Jesus heard the word that was spoken, he saith unto the ruler of the synagogue, Be not afraid, only believe.

**NKJV:** As soon as Jesus heard the word that was spoken, He said to the ruler of the synagogue, "Do not be afraid; only believe."

### Luke 1:74–75

**KJV:** That he would grant unto us, that we being delivered out of the hand of our enemies might serve him without fear, in holiness and righteousness before him, all the days of our life.

**NKJV:** To grant us that we, being delivered from the hand of our enemies, might serve Him without fear, in holiness and righteousness before Him all the days of our life.

### Luke 12:32

**KJV:** Fear not, little flock; for it is your Father's good pleasure to give you the kingdom.

**NKJV:** Do not fear, little flock, for it is your Father's good pleasure to give you the kingdom.

## Fear | Courage

### John 14:27

**KJV:** Peace I leave with you, my peace I give unto you: not as the world giveth, give I unto you. Let not your heart be troubled, neither let it be afraid.

**NKJV:** Peace I leave with you, My peace I give to you; not as the world gives do I give to you. Let not your heart be troubled, neither let it be afraid.

### Romans 8:15

**KJV:** For ye have not received the spirit of bondage again to fear; but ye have received the Spirit of adoption, whereby we cry, Abba, Father.

**NKJV:** For you did not receive the spirit of bondage again to fear, but you received the Spirit of adoption by whom we cry out, "Abba, Father."

### 2 Timothy 1:7

**KJV:** For God hath not given us the spirit of fear; but of power, and of love, and of a sound mind.

**NKJV:** For God has not given us a spirit of fear, but of power and of love and of a sound mind.

### Hebrews 2:14–15

**KJV:** Forasmuch then as the children are partakers of flesh and blood, he also himself likewise took part of the same; that through death he might destroy him that had the power of death, that is, the devil; and deliver them who through fear of death were all their lifetime subject to bondage.

**NKJV:** Inasmuch then as the children have partaken of flesh and blood, He Himself likewise shared in the same, that through death He might destroy him who had the power of death, that is, the devil, and release those who through fear of death were all their lifetime subject to bondage.

### Hebrews 13:5–6

**KJV:** Let your conversation be without covetousness; and be content with such things as ye have: for he hath said, I will never leave thee, nor forsake thee. So that we may boldly say, the Lord is my helper, and I will not fear what man shall do unto me.

**NKJV:** Let your conduct be without covetousness; be content with such things as you have. For He Himself has said, "I will never leave you nor forsake you." So we may boldly say: "The Lord is my helper; I will not fear. What can man do to me?"

### 1 John 4:18

**KJV:** There is no fear in love; but perfect love casteth out fear: because fear hath torment. He that feareth is not made perfect in love.

**NKJV:** There is no fear in love; but perfect love casts out fear, because fear involves torment. But he who fears has not been made perfect in love.

# 21 Fear of Man

> "Thank You, Father, that I trust
> in the LORD and am safe."
> Proverbs 29:25

### Proverbs 29:25

**KJV:** The fear of man bringeth a snare: but whoso putteth his trust in the LORD shall be safe.

**NKJV:** The fear of man brings a snare, but whoever trusts in the LORD shall be safe.

### Jeremiah 1:8

**KJV:** Be not afraid of their faces: for I am with thee to deliver thee, saith the LORD.

**NKJV:** "Do not be afraid of their faces, for I am with you to deliver you," says the LORD.

### John 16:22

**KJV:** And ye now therefore have sorrow: but I will see you again, and your heart shall rejoice, and your joy no man taketh from you.

**NKJV:** Therefore you now have sorrow; but I will see you again and your heart will rejoice, and your joy no one will take from you.

### Acts 26:17

**KJV:** Delivering thee from the people, and from the Gentiles, unto whom now I send thee.

**NKJV:** I will deliver you from the Jewish people, as well as from the Gentiles, to whom I now send you.

### 1 Corinthians 7:23

**KJV:** Ye are bought with a price; be not ye the servants of men.

**NKJV:** You were bought at a price; do not become slaves of men.

### 1 Corinthians 9:19

**KJV:** For though I be free from all men, yet have I made myself servant unto all, that I might gain the more.

**NKJV:** For though I am free from all men, I have made myself a servant to all, that I might win the more.

### Colossians 3:23

**KJV:** And whatsoever ye do, do it heartily, as to the Lord, and not unto men.

**NKJV:** And whatever you do, do it heartily, as to the Lord and not to men.

### 1 Thessalonians 2:4

**KJV:** But as we were allowed of God to be put in trust with the gospel, even so we speak; not as pleasing men, but God, which trieth our hearts.

**NKJV:** But as we have been approved by God to be entrusted with the gospel, even so we speak, not as pleasing men, but God who tests our hearts.

Pray the Word

# 22

## Finances

> "Thank You, Father, that today I give, and You give back to me good measure, pressed down and shaken together."
> Luke 6:38

### Deuteronomy 8:18

**KJV:** But thou shalt remember the Lord thy God: for it is he that giveth thee power to get wealth, that he may establish his covenant which he sware unto thy fathers, as it is this day.

**NKJV:** And you shall remember the Lord your God, for it is He who gives you power to get wealth, that He may establish His covenant which He swore to your fathers, as it is this day.

### Joshua 1:8

**KJV:** This book of the law shall not depart out of thy mouth; but thou shalt meditate therein day and night, that thou mayest observe to do according to all that is written therein: for then thou shalt make thy way prosperous, and then thou shalt have good success.

**NKJV:** This Book of the Law shall not depart from your mouth, but you shall meditate in it day and night, that you may observe to do according to all that is written in it. For then you will make your way prosperous, and then you will have good success.

### Psalm 1:3

**KJV:** And he shall be like a tree planted by the rivers of water, that bringeth forth his fruit in his season; his leaf also shall not wither; and whatsoever he doeth shall prosper.

**NKJV:** He shall be like a tree planted by the rivers of water, that brings forth its fruit in its season, whose leaf also shall not wither; and whatever he does shall prosper.

### Psalm 35:27

**KJV:** Let them shout for joy, and be glad, that favour my righteous cause: yea, let them say continually, Let the Lord be magnified, which hath pleasure in the prosperity of his servant.

**NKJV:** Let them shout for joy and be glad, who favor my righteous cause; And let them say continually, "Let the Lord be magnified, Who has pleasure in the prosperity of His servant."

### Psalm 112:1–3

**KJV:** Praise ye the Lord. Blessed is the man that feareth the Lord, that delighteth greatly in his commandments. His seed shall be mighty upon earth: the generation of the upright shall be blessed. Wealth and riches shall be in his house: and his righteousness endureth for ever.

**NKJV:** Praise the Lord! Blessed is the man who fears the Lord, Who delights greatly in His commandments. His descendants will be mighty on earth; the generation of the upright will be blessed. Wealth and riches will be in his house, and his righteousness endures forever.

### Psalm 115:14

**KJV:** The Lord shall increase you more and more, you and your children.

**NKJV:** May the Lord give you increase more and more, you and your children.

### Proverbs 3:9–10

**KJV:** Honour the Lord with thy substance, and with the firstfruits of all thine increase: so shall thy barns be filled with plenty, and thy presses shall burst out with new wine.

**NKJV:** Honor the Lord with your possessions, and with the firstfruits of all your increase; so your barns will be filled with plenty, and your vats will overflow with new wine.

### Proverbs 10:4

**KJV:** He becometh poor that dealeth with a slack hand: but the hand of the diligent maketh rich.

**NKJV:** He who has a slack hand becomes poor, but the hand of the diligent makes rich.

### Proverbs 10:22

**KJV:** The blessing of the Lord, it maketh rich, and he addeth no sorrow with it.

**NKJV:** The blessing of the Lord makes one rich, and He adds no sorrow with it.

### Proverbs 11:24–25

**KJV:** There is that scattereth, and yet increaseth; and there is that withholdeth more than is meet, but it tendeth to poverty. The liberal soul shall be made fat: and he that watereth shall be watered also himself.

**NKJV:** There is one who scatters, yet increases more; and there is one who withholds more than is right, but it leads to poverty. The generous soul will be made rich, and he who waters will also be watered himself.

### Proverbs 21:5

**KJV:** The thoughts of the diligent tend only to plenteousness; but of every one that is hasty only to want.

**NKJV:** The plans of the diligent lead surely to plenty, but those of everyone who is hasty, surely to poverty.

### Proverbs 21:20

**KJV:** There is treasure to be desired and oil in the dwelling of the wise; but a foolish man spendeth it up.

**NKJV:** There is desirable treasure, and oil in the dwelling of the wise, but a foolish man squanders it.

### Proverbs 22:9

**KJV:** He that hath a bountiful eye shall be blessed; for he giveth of his bread to the poor.

**NKJV:** He who has a generous eye will be blessed, for he gives of his bread to the poor.

### Matthew 6:33

**KJV:** But seek ye first the kingdom of God, and his righteousness; and all these things shall be added unto you.

**NKJV:** But seek first the kingdom of God and His righteousness, and all these things shall be added to you.

### Luke 6:38

**KJV:** Give, and it shall be given unto you; good measure, pressed down, and shaken together, and running over, shall men give into your bosom. For with the same measure that ye mete withal it shall be measured to you again.

**NKJV:** Give, and it will be given to you: good measure, pressed down, shaken together, and running over will be put into your bosom. For with the same measure that you use, it will be measured back to you.

### 2 Corinthians 8:9

**KJV:** For ye know the grace of our Lord Jesus Christ, that, though he was rich, yet for your sakes he became poor, that ye through his poverty might be rich.

**NKJV:** For you know the grace of our Lord Jesus Christ, that though He was rich, yet for your sakes He became poor, that you through His poverty might become rich.

### 2 Corinthians 9:6–10

**KJV:** But this I say, He which soweth sparingly shall reap also sparingly; and he which soweth bountifully shall reap also bountifully. Every man according as he purposeth in his heart, so let him give; not grudgingly, or of necessity: for God loveth a cheerful giver. And God is able to make all grace abound toward you; that ye, always having all sufficiency in all things, may abound to every good work: (As it is written, He hath dispersed abroad; he hath given to the poor: his righteousness remaineth for ever. Now he that ministereth seed to the sower both minister bread for your food, and multiply your seed sown, and increase the fruits of your righteousness).

**NKJV:** But this I say: He who sows sparingly will also reap sparingly, and he who sows bountifully will also reap bountifully. So let each one give as he purposes in his heart, not grudgingly or of necessity; for God loves a cheerful giver. And God is able to make all grace abound toward you, that you, always having all sufficiency in all things, may have an abundance for every good work. As it is written: "He has dispersed abroad, He has given to the poor; His righteousness endures forever." Now may He who supplies seed to the sower, and bread for food, supply and multiply the seed you have sown and increase the fruits of your righteousness.

### Galatians 6:7

**KJV:** Be not deceived; God is not mocked: for whatsoever a man soweth, that shall he also reap.

**NKJV:** Do not be deceived, God is not mocked; for whatever a man sows, that he will also reap.

### Philippians 4:19

**KJV:** But my God shall supply all your need according to his riches in glory by Christ Jesus.

**NKJV:** And my God shall supply all your need according to His riches in glory by Christ Jesus.

### 2 Thessalonians 3:10

**KJV:** For even when we were with you, this we commanded you, that if any would not work, neither should he eat.

**NKJV:** For even when we were with you, we commanded you this: if anyone will not work, neither shall he eat.

# 23 Forgiveness

> "Thank You, Father, that today I forgive as You have forgiven me."
> Ephesians 4:32

### Psalm 103:17

**KJV:** But the mercy of the LORD is from everlasting to everlasting upon them that fear him, and his righteousness unto children's children.

**NKJV:** But the mercy of the LORD is from everlasting to everlasting on those who fear Him, and His righteousness to children's children.

### Isaiah 1:18

**KJV:** Come now, and let us reason together, saith the LORD: though your sins be as scarlet, they shall be as white as snow; though they be red like crimson, they shall be as wool.

**NKJV:** "Come now, and let us reason together," says the Lord, "Though your sins are like scarlet, they shall be as white as snow; though they are red like crimson, they shall be as wool."

### Isaiah 43:25–26

**KJV:** I, even I, am he that blotteth out thy transgressions for mine own sake, and will not remember thy sins. Put me in remembrance: let us plead together: declare thou, that thou mayest be justified.

**NKJV:** I, even I, am He who blots out your transgressions for My own sake; and I will not remember your sins. Put Me in remembrance; let us contend together; state your case, that you may be acquitted.

### Micah 7:18–19

**KJV:** Who is a God like unto thee, that pardoneth iniquity, and passeth by the transgression of the remnant of his heritage? He retaineth not his anger for ever, because he delighteth in mercy. He will turn again, he will have compassion upon us; he will subdue our iniquities; and thou wilt cast all their sins into the depths of the sea.

**NKJV:** Who is a God like You, pardoning iniquity and passing over the transgression of the remnant of His heritage? He does not retain His anger forever, because He delights in mercy. He will again have compassion on us, and will subdue our iniquities. You will cast all our sins into the depths of the sea.

### Matthew 5:44

**KJV:** But I say unto you, love your enemies, bless them that curse you, do good to them that hate you, and pray for them which despitefully use you, and persecute you.

**NKJV:** But I say to you, love your enemies, bless those who curse you, do good to those who hate you, and pray for those who spitefully use you and persecute you.

## Forgiveness

### Matthew 6:14–15

**KJV:** For if ye forgive men their trespasses, your heavenly Father will also forgive you: but if ye forgive not men their trespasses, neither will your Father forgive your trespasses.

**NKJV:** For if you forgive men their trespasses, your heavenly Father will also forgive you. But if you do not forgive men their trespasses, neither will your Father forgive your trespasses.

### Mark 11:25

**KJV:** And when ye stand praying, forgive, if ye have ought against any: that your Father also which is in heaven may forgive you your trespasses.

**NKJV:** And whenever you stand praying, if you have anything against anyone, forgive him, that your Father in heaven may also forgive you your trespasses.

### Luke 23:34

**KJV:** Then said Jesus, Father, forgive them; for they know not what they do.

**NKJV:** Then Jesus said, "Father, forgive them, for they do not know what they do."

### Romans 12:14

**KJV:** Bless them which persecute you: bless, and curse not.

**NKJV:** Bless those who persecute you; bless and do not curse.

### Romans 12:18

**KJV:** If it be possible, as much as lieth in you, live peaceably with all men.

**NKJV:** If it is possible, as much as depends on you, live peaceably with all men.

### Ephesians 1:7
**KJV:** In whom we have redemption through his blood, the forgiveness of sins, according to the riches of his grace.

**NKJV:** In Him we have redemption through His blood, the forgiveness of sins, according to the riches of His grace.

### Ephesians 4:32
**KJV:** And be ye kind one to another, tenderhearted, forgiving one another, even as God for Christ's sake hath forgiven you.

**NKJV:** And be kind to one another, tenderhearted, forgiving one another, even as God in Christ forgave you.

### Colossians 1:14
**KJV:** In whom we have redemption through his blood, even the forgiveness of sins.

**NKJV:** In whom we have redemption through His blood, the forgiveness of sins.

### Colossians 3:13
**KJV:** Forbearing one another, and forgiving one another, if any man have a quarrel against any: even as Christ forgave you, so also do ye.

**NKJV:** Bearing with one another, and forgiving one another, if anyone has a complaint against another; even as Christ forgave you, so you also must do.

### 2 Timothy 4:16
**KJV:** At my first answer no man stood with me, but all men forsook me: I pray God that it may not be laid to their charge.

**NKJV:** At my first defense no one stood with me, but all forsook me. May it not be charged against them.

### Hebrews 8:12

**KJV:** For I will be merciful to their unrighteousness, and their sins and their iniquities will I remember no more.

**NKJV:** For I will be merciful to their unrighteousness, and their sins and their lawless deeds I will remember no more.

### 1 John 1:9

**KJV:** If we confess our sins, he is faithful and just to forgive us our sins, and to cleanse us from all unrighteousness.

**NKJV:** If we confess our sins, He is faithful and just to forgive us our sins and to cleanse us from all unrighteousness.

# Pray the Word

# 24 Friends

> "Thank You, Father, that I am a friend who loves at all times."
> Proverbs 17:17

### 2 Kings 2:2

**KJV:** And Elijah said unto Elisha, Tarry here, I pray thee; for the LORD hath sent me to Beth-el. And Elisha said unto him, As the LORD liveth, and as thy soul liveth, I will not leave thee. So they went down to Beth-el.

**NKJV:** Then Elijah said to Elisha, "Stay here, please, for the LORD has sent me on to Bethel." But Elisha said, "As the LORD lives, and as your soul lives, I will not leave you!" So they went down to Bethel.

### Proverbs 13:20

**KJV:** He that walketh with wise men shall be wise: but a companion of fools shall be destroyed.

**NKJV:** He who walks with wise men will be wise, but the companion of fools will be destroyed.

### Proverbs 12:26

**KJV:** The righteous is more excellent than his neighbour: but the way of the wicked seduceth them.

**NKJV:** The righteous should choose his friends carefully, for the way of the wicked leads them astray.

### Proverbs 17:17

**KJV:** A friend loveth at all times, and a brother is born for adversity.

**NKJV:** A friend loves at all times, and a brother is born for adversity.

### Proverbs 18:24

**KJV:** A man that hath friends must shew himself friendly: and there is a friend that sticketh closer than a brother.

**NKJV:** A man who has friends must himself be friendly, but there is a friend who sticks closer than a brother.

### Proverbs 22:24–25

**KJV:** Make no friendship with an angry man; and with a furious man thou shalt not go: lest thou learn his ways, and get a snare to thy soul.

**NKJV:** Make no friendship with an angry man, and with a furious man do not go, lest you learn his ways and set a snare for your soul.

### Proverbs 27:5–6

**KJV:** Open rebuke is better than secret love. Faithful are the wounds of a friend; but the kisses of an enemy are deceitful.

**NKJV:** Open rebuke is better than love carefully concealed. Faithful are the wounds of a friend, but the kisses of an enemy are deceitful.

### Proverbs 27:17

**KJV:** Iron sharpeneth iron; so a man sharpeneth the countenance of his friend.

**NKJV:** As iron sharpens iron, so a man sharpens the countenance of his friend.

### Ecclesiastes 4:9–10

**KJV:** Two are better than one; because they have a good reward for their labour. For if they fall, the one will lift up his fellow: but woe to him that is alone when he falleth; for he hath not another to help him up.

**NKJV:** Two are better than one, because they have a good reward for their labor. For if they fall, one will lift up his companion. But woe to him who is alone when he falls, for he has no one to help him up.

### John 15:13–15

**KJV:** Greater love hath no man than this, that a man lay down his life for his friends. Ye are my friends, if ye do whatsoever I command you. Henceforth I call you not servants; for the servant knoweth not what his lord doeth: but I have called you friends; for all things that I have heard of my Father I have made known unto you.

**NKJV:** Greater love has no one than this, than to lay down one's life for his friends. You are My friends if you do whatever I command you. No longer do I call you servants, for a servant does not know what his master is doing; but I have called you friends, for all things that I heard from My Father I have made known to you.

### 1 Corinthians 15:33

**KJV:** Be not deceived: evil communications corrupt good manners.

**NKJV:** Do not be deceived: "Evil company corrupts good habits."

### Colossians 3:12–14

**KJV:** Put on therefore, as the elect of God, holy and beloved, bowels of mercies, kindness, humbleness of mind, meekness, longsuffering; forbearing one another, and forgiving one another, if any man have a quarrel against any: even as Christ forgave you, so also do ye. And above all these things put on charity, which is the bond of perfectness.

**NKJV:** Therefore, as the elect of God, holy and beloved, put on tender mercies, kindness, humility, meekness, longsuffering; bearing with one another, and forgiving one another, if anyone has a complaint against another; even as Christ forgave you, so you also must do. But above all these things put on love, which is the bond of perfection.

# 25 Grace

> "Thank You, Father, that today I can come boldly to the throne of grace to obtain mercy and find grace in my time of need."
> Hebrews 4:16

### Romans 3:24

**KJV:** Being justified freely by his grace through the redemption that is in Christ Jesus.

**NKJV:** Being justified freely by His grace through the redemption that is in Christ Jesus.

### Romans 4:16

**KJV:** Therefore it is of faith, that it might be by grace; to the end the promise might be sure to all the seed; not to that only which is of the law, but to that also which is of the faith of Abraham; who is the father of us all.

**NKJV:** Therefore it is of faith that it might be according to grace, so that the promise might be sure to all the seed, not only to those who are of the law, but also to those who are of the faith of Abraham, who is the father of us all.

### Romans 6:14

**KJV:** For sin shall not have dominion over you: for ye are not under the law, but under grace.

**NKJV:** For sin shall not have dominion over you, for you are not under law but under grace.

### Romans 11:6

**KJV:** And if by grace, then is it no more of works: otherwise grace is no more grace. But if it be of works, then is it no more grace: otherwise work is no more work.

**NKJV:** And if by grace, then it is no longer of works; otherwise grace is no longer grace. But if it is of works, it is no longer grace; otherwise work is no longer work.

### Hebrews 4:16

**KJV:** Let us therefore come boldly unto the throne of grace, that we may obtain mercy, and find grace to help in time of need.

**NKJV:** Let us therefore come boldly to the throne of grace, that we may obtain mercy and find grace to help in time of need.

### Hebrews 13:9a

**KJV:** Be not carried about with divers and strange doctrines. For it is a good thing that the heart be established with grace.

**NKJV:** Do not be carried about with various and strange doctrines. For it is good that the heart be established by grace.

### James 4:6

**KJV:** But he giveth more grace. Wherefore he saith, God resisteth the proud, but giveth grace unto the humble.

**NKJV:** But He gives more grace. Therefore He says: "God resists the proud, But gives grace to the humble."

### 2 Peter 1:2

**KJV:** Grace and peace be multiplied unto you through the knowledge of God, and of Jesus our Lord.

**NKJV:** Grace and peace be multiplied to you in the knowledge of God and of Jesus our Lord.

Pray the Word

# 26 Grief

> "Thank You, Father, that You bind up
> my wounds and heal my broken heart."
> Psalm 147:3

### Joshua 1:9

**KJV:** Have not I commanded thee? Be strong and of a good courage; be not afraid, neither be thou dismayed: for the Lord thy God is with thee whithersoever thou goest.

**NKJV:** Have I not commanded you? Be strong and of good courage; do not be afraid, nor be dismayed, for the Lord your God is with you wherever you go.

### Psalm 31:24

**KJV:** Be of good courage, and he shall strengthen your heart, all ye that hope in the Lord.

**NKJV:** Be of good courage, and He shall strengthen your heart, all you who hope in the LORD.

### Psalm 34:18

**KJV:** The LORD is nigh unto them that are of a broken heart; and saveth such as be of a contrite spirit.

**NKJV:** The LORD is near to those who have a broken heart, and saves such as have a contrite spirit.

### Psalm 147:3

**KJV:** He healeth the broken in heart, and bindeth up their wounds.

**NKJV:** He heals the brokenhearted and binds up their wounds.

### Matthew 5:4

**KJV:** Blessed are they that mourn: for they shall be comforted.

**NKJV:** Blessed are those who mourn, for they shall be comforted.

### John 11:25–26

**KJV:** Jesus said unto her, I am the resurrection, and the life: he that believeth in me, though he were dead, yet shall he live: and whosoever liveth and believeth in me shall never die. Believest thou this?

**NKJV:** Jesus said to her, "I am the resurrection and the life. He who believes in Me, though he may die, he shall live. And whoever lives and believes in Me shall never die. Do you believe this?"

### John 14:1–2

**KJV:** Let not your heart be troubled: ye believe in God, believe also in me. In my Father's house are many mansions: if it were not so, I would have told you. I go to prepare a place for you.

**NKJV:** Let not your heart be troubled; you believe in God, believe also in Me. In My Father's house are many mansions; if it were not so, I would have told you. I go to prepare a place for you.

### 1 Corinthians 15:42–44

**KJV:** So also is the resurrection of the dead. It is sown in corruption; it is raised in incorruption: it is sown in dishonour; it is raised in glory: it is sown in weakness; it is raised in power: it is sown a natural body; it is raised a spiritual body. There is a natural body, and there is a spiritual body.

**NKJV:** So also is the resurrection of the dead. The body is sown in corruption, it is raised in incorruption. It is sown in dishonor, it is raised in glory. It is sown in weakness, it is raised in power. It is sown a natural body, it is raised a spiritual body. There is a natural body, and there is a spiritual body.

### 2 Corinthians 1:3–4

**KJV:** Blessed be God, even the Father of our Lord Jesus Christ, the Father of mercies, and the God of all comfort; who comforteth us in all our tribulation, that we may be able to comfort them which are in any trouble, by the comfort wherewith we ourselves are comforted of God.

**NKJV:** Blessed be the God and Father of our Lord Jesus Christ, the Father of mercies and God of all comfort, who comforts us in all our tribulation, that we may be able to comfort those who are in any trouble, with the comfort with which we ourselves are comforted by God.

### 2 Corinthians 5:8

**KJV:** We are confident, I say, and willing rather to be absent from the body, and to be present with the Lord.

**NKJV:** We are confident, yes, well pleased rather to be absent from the body and to be present with the Lord.

## Pray the Word

### 1 Thessalonians 4:14–18

**KJV:** For if we believe that Jesus died and rose again, even so them also which sleep in Jesus will God bring with him. For this we say unto you by the word of the Lord, that we which are alive and remain unto the coming of the Lord shall not prevent them which are asleep. For the Lord himself shall descend from heaven with a shout, with the voice of the archangel, and with the trump of God: and the dead in Christ shall rise first: then we which are alive and remain shall be caught up together with them in the clouds, to meet the Lord in the air: and so shall we ever be with the Lord. Wherefore comfort one another with these words.

**NKJV:** For if we believe that Jesus died and rose again, even so God will bring with Him those who sleep in Jesus. For this we say to you by the word of the Lord, that we who are alive and remain until the coming of the Lord will by no means precede those who are asleep. For the Lord Himself will descend from heaven with a shout, with the voice of an archangel, and with the trumpet of God. And the dead in Christ will rise first. Then we who are alive and remain shall be caught up together with them in the clouds to meet the Lord in the air. And thus we shall always be with the Lord. Therefore comfort one another with these words.

### Revelation 21:4

**KJV:** And God shall wipe away all tears from their eyes; and there shall be no more death, neither sorrow, nor crying, neither shall there be any more pain: for the former things are passed away.

**NKJV:** And God will wipe away every tear from their eyes; there shall be no more death, nor sorrow, nor crying. There shall be no more pain, for the former things have passed away.

### Revelation 14:13

**KJV:** And I heard a voice from heaven saying unto me, Write, Blessed are the dead which die in the Lord from henceforth: Yea, saith the Spirit, that they may rest from their labours; and their works do follow them.

**NKJV:** Then I heard a voice from heaven saying to me, "Write: 'Blessed are the dead who die in the Lord from now on.'" "Yes," says the Spirit, "that they may rest from their labors, and their works follow them."

Pray the Word

# 27 Guilt

> "Thank You, Father, that there is no condemnation toward those who are in Christ Jesus."
> Romans 8:1

### Psalm 103:12

**KJV:** As far as the east is from the west, so far hath he removed our transgressions from us.

**NKJV:** As far as the east is from the west, so far has He removed our transgressions from us.

### Proverbs 28:13

**KJV:** He that covereth his sins shall not prosper: but whoso confesseth and forsaketh them shall have mercy.

**NKJV:** He who covers his sins will not prosper, but whoever confesses and forsakes them will have mercy.

### Isaiah 1:18

**KJV:** Come now, and let us reason together, saith the LORD: though your sins be as scarlet, they shall be as white as snow; though they be red like crimson, they shall be as wool.

**NKJV:** "Come now, and let us reason together," says the LORD, "Though your sins are like scarlet, they shall be as white as snow; though they are red like crimson, they shall be as wool."

### Isaiah 43:25

**KJV:** I, even I, am He who blots out your transgressions for My own sake; and I will not remember your sins.

**NKJV:** I, even I, am he that blotteth out thy transgressions for mine own sake, and will not remember thy sins.

### Romans 5:1

**KJV:** Therefore being justified by faith, we have peace with God through our Lord Jesus Christ:

**NKJV:** Therefore, having been justified by faith, we have peace with God through our Lord Jesus Christ,

### Romans 5:20

**KJV:** Moreover the law entered, that the offence might abound. But where sin abounded, grace did much more abound:

**NKJV:** Moreover the law entered that the offense might abound. But where sin abounded, grace abounded much more,

### Romans 8:1

**KJV:** There is therefore now no condemnation to them which are in Christ Jesus, who walk not after the flesh, but after the Spirit.

**NKJV:** There is therefore now no condemnation to those who are in Christ Jesus, who do not walk according to the flesh, but according to the Spirit.

### Romans 8:33

**KJV:** Who shall lay any thing to the charge of God's elect? It is God that justifieth.

**NKJV:** Who shall bring a charge against God's elect? It is God who justifies.

### 2 Corinthians 5:17

**KJV:** Therefore if any man be in Christ, he is a new creature: old things are passed away; behold, all things are become new.

**NKJV:** Therefore, if anyone is in Christ, he is a new creation; old things have passed away; behold, all things have become new.

### 2 Corinthians 5:21

**KJV:** For he hath made him to be sin for us, who knew no sin; that we might be made the righteousness of God in him.

**NKJV:** For He made Him who knew no sin to be sin for us, that we might become the righteousness of God in Him.

### Philippians 3:13–14

**KJV:** Brethren, I count not myself to have apprehended: but this one thing I do, forgetting those things which are behind, and reaching forth unto those things which are before, I press toward the mark for the prize of the high calling of God in Christ Jesus.

**NKJV:** Brethren, I do not count myself to have apprehended; but one thing I do, forgetting those things which are behind and reaching forward to those things which are ahead, I press toward the goal for the prize of the upward call of God in Christ Jesus.

### Hebrews 8:12

**KJV:** For I will be merciful to their unrighteousness, and their sins and their iniquities will I remember no more.

**NKJV:** For I will be merciful to their unrighteousness, and their sins and their lawless deeds I will remember no more.

### Hebrews 10:22

**KJV:** Let us draw near with a true heart in full assurance of faith, having our hearts sprinkled from an evil conscience, and our bodies washed with pure water.

**NKJV:** Let us draw near with a true heart in full assurance of faith, having our hearts sprinkled from an evil conscience and our bodies washed with pure water.

### 1 John 1:9

**KJV:** If we confess our sins, he is faithful and just to forgive us our sins, and to cleanse us from all unrighteousness.

**NKJV:** If we confess our sins, He is faithful and just to forgive us our sins and to cleanse us from all unrighteousness.

# 20 Healing Health

> "Thank You, Father, that today
> I receive what belongs to me:
> 'By His stripes I was healed.'"
> 1 Peter 2:24

### Exodus 23:25–26

**KJV:** And ye shall serve the Lord your God, and he shall bless thy bread, and thy water; and I will take sickness away from the midst of thee. There shall nothing cast their young, nor be barren, in thy land: the number of thy days I will fulfil.

**NKJV:** So you shall serve the Lord your God, and He will bless your bread and your water. And I will take sickness away from the midst of you. No one shall suffer miscarriage or be barren in your land; I will fulfill the number of your days.

## Pray the Word

### Deuteronomy 7:15a

**KJV:** And the L<small>ORD</small> will take away from thee all sickness, and will put none of the evil diseases of Egypt, which thou knowest, upon thee.

**NKJV:** And the L<small>ORD</small> will take away from you all sickness, and will afflict you with none of the terrible diseases of Egypt which you have known.

### Psalm 30:2

**KJV:** O L<small>ORD</small> my God, I cried unto thee, and thou hast healed me.

**NKJV:** O L<small>ORD</small> my God, I cried out to You, and You healed me.

### Psalm 91:10

**KJV:** There shall no evil befall thee, neither shall any plague come nigh thy dwelling.

**NKJV:** No evil shall befall you, nor shall any plague come near your dwelling;

### Psalm 103:1–5

**KJV:** Bless the L<small>ORD</small>, O my soul: and all that is within me, bless his holy name. Bless the L<small>ORD</small>, O my soul, and forget not all his benefits: who forgiveth all thine iniquities; who healeth all thy diseases; who redeemeth thy life from destruction; who crowneth thee with lovingkindness and tender mercies; who satisfieth thy mouth with good things; so that thy youth is renewed like the eagle's.

**NKJV:** Bless the L<small>ORD</small>, O my soul; and all that is within me, bless His holy name! Bless the L<small>ORD</small>, O my soul, and forget not all His benefits: who forgives all your iniquities, who heals all your diseases, who redeems your life from destruction, who crowns you with lovingkindness and tender mercies, who satisfies your mouth with good things, so that your youth is renewed like the eagle's.

## Healing | Health

### Psalm 105:37

**KJV:** He brought them forth also with silver and gold: and there was not one feeble person among their tribes.

**NKJV:** He also brought them out with silver and gold, and there was none feeble among His tribes.

### Psalm 107:20

**KJV:** He sent his word, and healed them, and delivered them from their destructions.

**NKJV:** He sent His word and healed them, and delivered them from their destructions.

### Proverbs 3:7–8

**KJV:** Be not wise in thine own eyes: fear the Lord, and depart from evil. It shall be health to thy navel, and marrow to thy bones.

**NKJV:** Do not be wise in your own eyes; fear the Lord and depart from evil. It will be health to your flesh, and strength to your bones.

### Proverbs 4:20–23

**KJV:** My son, attend to my words; incline thine ear unto my sayings. Let them not depart from thine eyes; keep them in the midst of thine heart. For they are life unto those that find them, and health to all their flesh. Keep thy heart with all diligence; for out of it are the issues of life.

**NKJV:** My son, give attention to my words; Incline your ear to my sayings. Do not let them depart from your eyes; keep them in the midst of your heart; for they are life to those who find them, and health to all their flesh. Keep your heart with all diligence, for out of it spring the issues of life.

### Proverbs 18:14

**KJV:** The spirit of a man will sustain his infirmity; but a wounded spirit who can bear?

**NKJV:** The spirit of a man will sustain him in sickness, but who can bear a broken spirit?

### Isaiah 53:4–5

**KJV:** Surely he hath borne our griefs, and carried our sorrows: yet we did esteem him stricken, smitten of God, and afflicted. But he was wounded for our transgressions, he was bruised for our iniquities: the chastisement of our peace was upon him; and with his stripes we are healed.

**NKJV:** Surely He has borne our griefs and carried our sorrows; Yet we esteemed Him stricken, Smitten by God, and afflicted. But He was wounded for our transgressions, He was bruised for our iniquities; the chastisement for our peace was upon Him, and by His stripes we are healed.

### Isaiah 58:8

**KJV:** Then shall thy light break forth as the morning, and thine health shall spring forth speedily: and thy righteousness shall go before thee; the glory of the Lord shall be thy reward.

**NKJV:** Then your light shall break forth like the morning, your healing shall spring forth speedily, and your righteousness shall go before you; the glory of the Lord shall be your rear guard.

### Jeremiah 30:17

**KJV:** For I will restore health unto thee, and I will heal thee of thy wounds, saith the Lord; because they called thee an outcast, saying, This is Zion, whom no man seeketh after.

## Healing | Health

**NKJV:** "For I will restore health to you and heal you of your wounds," says the Lord, "Because they called you an outcast saying: 'This is Zion; No one seeks her.'"

### Jeremiah 33:6

**KJV:** Behold, I will bring it health and cure, and I will cure them, and will reveal unto them the abundance of peace and truth.

**NKJV:** Behold, I will bring it health and healing; I will heal them and reveal to them the abundance of peace and truth.

### Malachi 4:2

**KJV:** But unto you that fear my name shall the Sun of righteousness arise with healing in his wings; and ye shall go forth, and grow up as calves of the stall.

**NKJV:** But to you who fear My name the Sun of Righteousness shall arise with healing in His wings; and you shall go out and grow fat like stall-fed calves.

### Matthew 8:17

**KJV:** That it might be fulfilled which was spoken by Esaias the prophet, saying, Himself took our infirmities, and bare our sicknesses.

**NKJV:** That it might be fulfilled which was spoken by Isaiah the prophet, saying: "He Himself took our infirmities and bore our sicknesses."

### Mark 5:34

**KJV:** And he said unto her, Daughter, thy faith hath made thee whole; go in peace, and be whole of thy plague.

**NKJV:** And He said to her, "Daughter, your faith has made you well. Go in peace, and be healed of your affliction."

### Romans 8:11

**KJV:** But if the Spirit of him that raised up Jesus from the dead dwell in you, he that raised up Christ from the dead shall also quicken your mortal bodies by his Spirit that dwelleth in you.

**NKJV:** But if the Spirit of Him who raised Jesus from the dead dwells in you, He who raised Christ from the dead will also give life to your mortal bodies through His Spirit who dwells in you.

### Galatians 3:13

**KJV:** Christ hath redeemed us from the curse of the law, being made a curse for us: for it is written, Cursed is every one that hangeth on a tree:

**NKJV:** Christ has redeemed us from the curse of the law, having become a curse for us (for it is written, "Cursed is everyone who hangs on a tree").

### 1 Peter 2:24

**KJV:** Who his own self bare our sins in his own body on the tree, that we, being dead to sins, should live unto righteousness: by whose stripes ye were healed.

**NKJV:** Who Himself bore our sins in His own body on the tree, that we, having died to sins, might live for righteousness—by whose stripes you were healed.

### 3 John 2

**KJV:** Beloved, I wish above all things that thou mayest prosper and be in health, even as thy soul prospereth.

**NKJV:** Beloved, I pray that you may prosper in all things and be in health, just as your soul prospers.

# 29 Honesty

> "Thank You, Father, that I provide things honest in the sight of God and man."
> 2 Corinthians 8:21

### Proverbs 10:9

**KJV:** He that walketh uprightly walketh surely: but he that perverteth his ways shall be known.

**NKJV:** He who walks with integrity walks securely, but he who perverts his ways will become known.

### Proverbs 11:3

**KJV:** The integrity of the upright shall guide them: but the perverseness of transgressors shall destroy them.

**NKJV:** The integrity of the upright will guide them, but the perversity of the unfaithful will destroy them.

### Proverbs 12:22

**KJV:** Lying lips are abomination to the Lord: but they that deal truly are his delight.

**NKJV:** Lying lips are an abomination to the Lord, but those who deal truthfully are His delight.

### Proverbs 14:5

**KJV:** A faithful witness will not lie: but a false witness will utter lies.

**NKJV:** A faithful witness does not lie, but a false witness will utter lies.

### Proverbs 24:26

**KJV:** Every man shall kiss his lips that giveth a right answer.

**NKJV:** He who gives a right answer kisses the lips.

### Proverbs 28:18

**KJV:** Whoso walketh uprightly shall be saved: but he that is perverse in his ways shall fall at once.

**NKJV:** Whoever walks blamelessly will be saved, but he who is perverse in his ways will suddenly fall.

### Matthew 5:8

**KJV:** Blessed are the pure in heart: for they shall see God.

**NKJV:** Blessed are the pure in heart, for they shall see God.

### 2 Corinthians 8:21

**KJV:** Providing for honest things, not only in the sight of the Lord, but also in the sight of men.

**NKJV:** Providing honorable things, not only in the sight of the Lord, but also in the sight of men.

### Ephesians 4:25

**KJV:** Wherefore putting away lying, speak every man truth with his neighbour: for we are members one of another.

**NKJV:** Therefore, putting away lying, "Let each one of you speak truth with his neighbor," for we are members of one another.

### Colossians 3:9

**KJV:** Lie not one to another, seeing that ye have put off the old man with his deeds.

**NKJV:** Do not lie to one another, since you have put off the old man with his deeds.

### 1 Peter 3:10

**KJV:** For he that will love life, and see good days, let him refrain his tongue from evil, and his lips that they speak no guile.

**NKJV:** For "He who would love life and see good days, let him refrain his tongue from evil, and his lips from speaking deceit."

### 1 John 3:18

**KJV:** My little children, let us not love in word, neither in tongue; but in deed and in truth.

**NKJV:** My little children, let us not love in word or in tongue, but in deed and in truth.

Pray the Word

# 30 Honor Respect

> "Thank You, Father, that today
> I do unto others as I would have
> them do unto me."
> Matthew 7:12

### Matthew 7:12

**KJV:** Therefore all things whatsoever ye would that men should do to you, do ye even so to them: for this is the law and the prophets.

**NKJV:** Therefore, whatever you want men to do to you, do also to them, for this is the Law and the Prophets.

### John 13:35

**KJV:** By this shall all men know that ye are my disciples, if ye have love one to another.

**NKJV:** By this all will know that you are My disciples, if you have love for one another.

### Romans 12:10

**KJV:** Be kindly affectioned one to another with brotherly love; in honour preferring one another.

**NKJV:** Be kindly affectionate to one another with brotherly love, in honor giving preference to one another.

### Romans 13:1

**KJV:** Let every soul be subject unto the higher powers. For there is no power but of God: the powers that be are ordained of God.

**NKJV:** Let every soul be subject to the governing authorities. For there is no authority except from God, and the authorities that exist are appointed by God.

### Ephesians 6:1–3

**KJV:** Children, obey your parents in the Lord: for this is right. Honour thy father and mother; (which is the first commandment with promise;) that it may be well with thee, and thou mayest live long on the earth.

**NKJV:** Children, obey your parents in the Lord, for this is right. "Honor your father and mother," which is the first commandment with promise: "that it may be well with you and you may live long on the earth."

### 1 Thessalonians 5:12–14

**KJV:** And we beseech you, brethren, to know them which labour among you, and are over you in the Lord, and admonish you; and to esteem them very highly in love for their work's sake. And be at peace among yourselves. Now we exhort you, brethren, warn them that are unruly, comfort the feebleminded, support the weak, be patient toward all men.

NKJV: And we urge you, brethren, to recognize those who labor among you, and are over you in the Lord and admonish you, and to esteem them very highly in love for their work's sake. Be at peace among yourselves. Now we exhort you, brethren, warn those who are unruly, comfort the fainthearted, uphold the weak, be patient with all.

### Hebrews 13:7

KJV: Remember them which have the rule over you, who have spoken unto you the word of God: whose faith follow, considering the end of their conversation.

NKJV: Remember those who rule over you, who have spoken the word of God to you, whose faith follow, considering the outcome of their conduct.

### Hebrews 13:17

KJV: Obey them that have the rule over you, and submit yourselves: for they watch for your souls, as they that must give account, that they may do it with joy, and not with grief: for that is unprofitable for you.

NKJV: Obey those who rule over you, and be submissive, for they watch out for your souls, as those who must give account. Let them do so with joy and not with grief, for that would be unprofitable for you.

### 1 Peter 2:17

KJV: Honour all men. Love the brotherhood. Fear God. Honour the king.

NKJV: Honor all people. Love the brotherhood. Fear God. Honor the king.

Pray the Word

# 31 Hope

> "Thank You, Father, that hope is an anchor to my soul today."
> Hebrews 6:19

### Psalm 3:3

**KJV:** But thou, O Lord, art a shield for me; my glory, and the lifter up of mine head.

**NKJV:** But You, O Lord, are a shield for me, my glory and the One who lifts up my head.

### Proverbs 13:12

**KJV:** Hope deferred maketh the heart sick: but when the desire cometh, it is a tree of life.

**NKJV:** Hope deferred makes the heart sick, but when the desire comes, it is a tree of life.

### Jeremiah 29:11

**KJV:** For I know the thoughts that I think toward you, saith the Lord, thoughts of peace, and not of evil, to give you an expected end.

**NKJV:** For I know the thoughts that I think toward you, says the Lord, thoughts of peace and not of evil, to give you a future and a hope.

### Zechariah 9:12

**KJV:** Turn you to the strong hold, ye prisoners of hope: even today do I declare that I will render double unto thee.

**NKJV:** Return to the stronghold, you prisoners of hope. Even today I declare that I will restore double to you.

### Romans 5:5

**KJV:** And hope maketh not ashamed; because the love of God is shed abroad in our hearts by the Holy Ghost which is given unto us.

**NKJV:** Now hope does not disappoint, because the love of God has been poured out in our hearts by the Holy Spirit who was given to us.

### 1 Corinthians 15:55–58

**KJV:** O death, where is thy sting? O grave, where is thy victory? The sting of death is sin; and the strength of sin is the law. But thanks be to God, which giveth us the victory through our Lord Jesus Christ. Therefore, my beloved brethren, be ye stedfast, unmoveable, always abounding in the work of the Lord, forasmuch as ye know that your labour is not in vain in the Lord.

**NKJV:** "O Death, where is your sting? O Hades, where is your victory?" The sting of death is sin, and the strength of sin is the law. But thanks be to God, who gives us the victory through our Lord Jesus Christ. Therefore, my beloved brethren, be steadfast, immovable, always abounding in the work of the Lord, knowing that your labor is not in vain in the Lord.

### Hebrews 6:19

**KJV:** Which hope we have as an anchor of the soul, both sure and stedfast, and which entereth into that within the veil.

**NKJV:** This hope we have as an anchor of the soul, both sure and steadfast, and which enters the presence behind the veil.

### Hebrews 11:1

**KJV:** Now faith is the substance of things hoped for, the evidence of things not seen.

**NKJV:** Now faith is the substance of things hoped for, the evidence of things not seen.

Pray the Word

# 32 Intimacy with God

> "Thank You, Father, that this is my purpose: to know God."
> Philippians 3:10

### Psalm 42:1–2

**KJV:** As the hart panteth after the water brooks, so panteth my soul after thee, O God. My soul thirsteth for God, for the living God: when shall I come and appear before God?

**NKJV:** As the deer pants for the water brooks, so pants my soul for You, O God. My soul thirsts for God, for the living God. When shall I come and appear before God?

### Psalm 43:4

**KJV:** Then will I go unto the altar of God, unto God my exceeding joy: yea, upon the harp will I praise thee, O God my God.

NKJV: Then I will go to the altar of God, to God my exceeding joy; and on the harp I will praise You, O God, my God.

### Psalm 43:5

KJV: Why art thou cast down, O my soul? And why art thou disquieted within me? Hope in God: for I shall yet praise him, who is the health of my countenance, and my God.

NKJV: Why are you cast down, O my soul? And why are you disquieted within me? Hope in God; for I shall yet praise Him, the help of my countenance and my God.

### Psalm 63:1

KJV: O God, thou art my God; early will I seek thee: my soul thirsteth for thee, my flesh longeth for thee in a dry and thirsty land, where no water is.

NKJV: O God, You are my God; early will I seek You; my soul thirsts for You; my flesh longs for You in a dry and thirsty land where there is no water.

### Psalm 63:5

KJV: My soul shall be satisfied as with marrow and fatness; and my mouth shall praise thee with joyful lips.

NKJV: My soul shall be satisfied as with marrow and fatness, and my mouth shall praise You with joyful lips.

### Psalm 63:8

KJV: My soul followeth hard after thee: thy right hand upholdeth me.

NKJV: My soul follows close behind You; Your right hand upholds me.

### Psalm 73:25

**KJV:** Whom have I in heaven but thee? And there is none upon earth that I desire beside thee.

**NKJV:** Whom have I in heaven but You? And there is none upon earth that I desire besides You.

### Psalm 85:6

**KJV:** Wilt thou not revive us again: that thy people may rejoice in thee?

**NKJV:** Will You not revive us again, that Your people may rejoice in You?

### Daniel 11:32

**KJV:** And such as do wickedly against the covenant shall he corrupt by flatteries: but the people that do know their God shall be strong, and do exploits.

**NKJV:** Those who do wickedly against the covenant he shall corrupt with flattery; but the people who know their God shall be strong, and carry out great exploits.

### Matthew 5:6

**KJV:** Blessed are they which do hunger and thirst after righteousness: for they shall be filled.

**NKJV:** Blessed are those who hunger and thirst for righteousness, for they shall be filled.

### Mark 3:13–15

**KJV:** And he goeth up into a mountain, and calleth unto him whom he would: and they came unto him. And he ordained twelve, that they should be with him, and that he might send them forth to preach, and to have power to heal sicknesses, and to cast out devils.

**NKJV:** And He went up on the mountain and called to Him those He Himself wanted. And they came to Him. Then He appointed twelve, that they might be with Him and that He might send them out to preach, and to have power to heal sicknesses and to cast out demons.

### John 6:35

**KJV:** And Jesus said unto them, I am the bread of life: he that cometh to me shall never hunger; and he that believeth on me shall never thirst.

**NKJV:** And Jesus said to them, "I am the bread of life. He who comes to Me shall never hunger, and he who believes in Me shall never thirst."

### Romans 12:11

**KJV:** Not slothful in business; fervent in spirit; serving the Lord.

**NKJV:** Not lagging in diligence, fervent in spirit, serving the Lord.

### 2 Corinthians 13:14

**KJV:** The grace of the Lord Jesus Christ, and the love of God, and the communion of the Holy Ghost, be with you all. Amen.

**NKJV:** The grace of the Lord Jesus Christ, and the love of God, and the communion of the Holy Spirit be with you all. Amen.

### Philippians 3:10

**KJV:** That I may know him, and the power of his resurrection, and the fellowship of his sufferings, being made conformable unto his death.

**NKJV:** That I may know Him and the power of His resurrection, and the fellowship of His sufferings, being conformed to His death.

### 2 Timothy 1:6

**KJV:** Wherefore I put thee in remembrance that thou stir up the gift of God, which is in thee by the putting on of my hands.

**NKJV:** Therefore I remind you to stir up the gift of God which is in you through the laying on of my hands.

### James 4:8

**KJV:** Draw nigh to God, and he will draw nigh to you. Cleanse your hands, ye sinners; and purify your hearts, ye double minded.

**NKJV:** Draw near to God and He will draw near to you. Cleanse your hands, you sinners; and purify your hearts, you double-minded.

Pray the Word

# Leadership

> "Thank You, Father, that I lead as a great servant today because I know that the greatest among us is the greatest servant."
> Mark 10:43

### Proverbs 22:29

**KJV:** Seest thou a man diligent in his business? He shall stand before kings; he shall not stand before mean men.

**NKJV:** Do you see a man who excels in his work? He will stand before kings; he will not stand before unknown men.

### Proverbs 27:23

**KJV:** Be thou diligent to know the state of thy flocks, and look well to thy herds.

**NKJV:** Be diligent to know the state of your flocks, and attend to your herds.

## Mark 10:43–45

**KJV:** But so shall it not be among you: but whosoever will be great among you, shall be your minister: and whosoever of you will be the chiefest, shall be servant of all. For even the Son of man came not to be ministered unto, but to minister, and to give his life a ransom for many.

**NKJV:** Yet it shall not be so among you; but whoever desires to become great among you shall be your servant. And whoever of you desires to be first shall be slave of all. For even the Son of Man did not come to be served, but to serve, and to give His life a ransom for many.

## Ephesians 4:11–16

**KJV:** And he gave some, apostles; and some, prophets; and some, evangelists; and some, pastors and teachers; for the perfecting of the saints, for the work of the ministry, for the edifying of the body of Christ: till we all come in the unity of the faith, and of the knowledge of the Son of God, unto a perfect man, unto the measure of the stature of the fulness of Christ: that we henceforth be no more children, tossed to and fro, and carried about with every wind of doctrine, by the sleight of men, and cunning craftiness, whereby they lie in wait to deceive; but speaking the truth in love, may grow up into him in all things, which is the head, even Christ: from whom the whole body fitly joined together and compacted by that which every joint supplieth, according to the effectual working in the measure of every part, maketh increase of the body unto the edifying of itself in love.

**NKJV:** And He Himself gave some to be apostles, some prophets, some evangelists, and some pastors and teachers, for the equipping of the saints for the work of ministry, for the edifying of the body of Christ, till we all come to the unity of the faith and of the knowledge of the Son of God, to a perfect man, to the measure of the stature of the fullness of Christ; that we should no longer be children, tossed to and fro and carried about with every wind of doctrine, by the trickery of men, in the cunning craftiness of deceitful plotting, but, speaking the truth in love, may grow up in all things into Him who is the head—Christ—from whom the whole body, joined and knit together by what every joint supplies, according to the effective working by which every part does its share, causes growth of the body for the edifying of itself in love.

### Philippians 2:3

**KJV:** Let nothing be done through strife or vainglory; but in lowliness of mind let each esteem other better than themselves.

**NKJV:** Let nothing be done through selfish ambition or conceit, but in lowliness of mind let each esteem others better than himself.

### Philippians 2:4

**KJV:** Look not every man on his own things, but every man also on the things of others.

**NKJV:** Let each of you look out not only for his own interests, but also for the interests of others.

### 1 Timothy 3:3

**KJV:** Not given to wine, no striker, not greedy of filthy lucre; but patient, not a brawler, not covetous.

**NKJV:** Not given to wine, not violent, not greedy for money, but gentle, not quarrelsome, not covetous.

### 1 Timothy 4:12

**KJV:** Let no man despise thy youth; but be thou an example of the believers, in word, in conversation, in charity, in spirit, in faith, in purity.

**NKJV:** Let no one despise your youth, but be an example to the believers in word, in conduct, in love, in spirit, in faith, in purity.

### 2 Timothy 2:15

**KJV:** Study to shew thyself approved unto God, a workman that needeth not to be ashamed, rightly dividing the word of truth.

**NKJV:** Be diligent to present yourself approved to God, a worker who does not need to be ashamed, rightly dividing the word of truth.

### Titus 1:9

**KJV:** Holding fast the faithful word as he hath been taught, that he may be able by sound doctrine both to exhort and to convince the gainsayers.

**NKJV:** Holding fast the faithful word as he has been taught, that he may be able, by sound doctrine, both to exhort and convict those who contradict.

### Hebrews 13:7

**KJV:** Remember them which have the rule over you, who have spoken unto you the word of God: whose faith follow, considering the end of their conversation.

**NKJV:** Remember those who rule over you, who have spoken the word of God to you, whose faith follow, considering the outcome of their conduct.

### 1 Peter 5:1–3

**KJV:** The elders which are among you I exhort, who am also an elder, and a witness of the sufferings of Christ, and also a partaker of the glory that shall be revealed: feed the flock of God which is among you, taking the oversight thereof, not by constraint, but willingly; not for filthy lucre, but of a ready mind; neither as being lords over God's heritage, but being ensamples to the flock.

**NKJV:** The elders who are among you I exhort, I who am a fellow elder and a witness of the sufferings of Christ, and also a partaker of the glory that will be revealed: shepherd the flock of God which is among you, serving as overseers, not by compulsion but willingly, not for dishonest gain but eagerly; nor as being lords over those entrusted to you, but being examples to the flock.

Pray the Word

# Loneliness

> "Thank You, Father, that You never leave me nor forsake me."
> Hebrews 13:5

### Deuteronomy 31:6

**KJV:** Be strong and of a good courage, fear not, nor be afraid of them: for the LORD thy God, he it is that doth go with thee; he will not fail thee, nor forsake thee.

**NKJV:** Be strong and of good courage, do not fear nor be afraid of them; for the LORD your God, He is the One who goes with you. He will not leave you nor forsake you.

### Psalm 27:10

**KJV:** When my father and my mother forsake me, then the LORD will take me up.

**NKJV:** When my father and my mother forsake me, then the Lord will take care of me.

### Psalm 68:5–6a

**KJV:** A father of the fatherless, and a judge of the widows, is God in his holy habitation. God setteth the solitary in families.

**NKJV:** A father of the fatherless, a defender of widows, is God in His holy habitation. God sets the solitary in families.

### Psalm 147:3

**KJV:** He healeth the broken in heart, and bindeth up their wounds.

**NKJV:** He heals the brokenhearted and binds up their wounds.

### Proverbs 8:31

**KJV:** Rejoicing in the habitable part of his earth; and my delights were with the sons of men.

**NKJV:** Rejoicing in His inhabited world, and my delight was with the sons of men.

### Proverbs 18:24

**KJV:** A man that hath friends must shew himself friendly: and there is a friend that sticketh closer than a brother.

**NKJV:** A man who has friends must himself be friendly, but there is a friend who sticks closer than a brother.

### Isaiah 41:10

**KJV:** Fear thou not; for I am with thee: be not dismayed; for I am thy God: I will strengthen thee; yea, I will help thee; yea, I will uphold thee with the right hand of my righteousness.

**NKJV:** Fear not, for I am with you; be not dismayed, for I am your God. I will strengthen you, yes, I will help you, I will uphold you with My righteous right hand.

### Matthew 28:20

**KJV:** Teaching them to observe all things whatsoever I have commanded you: and, lo, I am with you alway, even unto the end of the world. Amen.

**NKJV:** "Teaching them to observe all things that I have commanded you; and lo, I am with you always, even to the end of the age." Amen.

### Romans 8:35–39

**KJV:** Who shall separate us from the love of Christ? Shall tribulation, or distress, or persecution, or famine, or nakedness, or peril, or sword? As it is written, For thy sake we are killed all the day long; we are accounted as sheep for the slaughter. Nay, in all these things we are more than conquerors through him that loved us. For I am persuaded, that neither death, nor life, nor angels, nor principalities, nor powers, nor things present, nor things to come, Nor height, nor depth, nor any other creature, shall be able to separate us from the love of God, which is in Christ Jesus our Lord.

**NKJV:** Who shall separate us from the love of Christ? Shall tribulation, or distress, or persecution, or famine, or nakedness, or peril, or sword? As it is written: "For Your sake we are killed all day long; We are accounted as sheep for the slaughter." Yet in all these things we are more than conquerors through Him who loved us. For I am persuaded that neither death nor life, nor angels nor principalities nor powers, nor things present nor things to come, nor height nor depth, nor any other created thing, shall be able to separate us from the love of God which is in Christ Jesus our Lord.

# Pray the Word

### Hebrews 13:5–6

**KJV:** Let your conversation be without covetousness; and be content with such things as ye have: for he hath said, I will never leave thee, nor forsake thee. So that we may boldly say, The Lord is my helper, and I will not fear what man shall do unto me.

**NKJV:** Let your conduct be without covetousness; be content with such things as you have. For He Himself has said, "I will never leave you nor forsake you." So we may boldly say: "The Lord is my helper; I will not fear. What can man do to me?"

# 35 Long Life

> "Thank You, Father, that You satisfy me with long life."
> Psalm 91:16

### Genesis 25:8

**KJV:** Then Abraham gave up the ghost, and died in a good old age, an old man, and full of years; and was gathered to his people.

**NKJV:** Then Abraham breathed his last and died in a good old age, an old man and full of years, and was gathered to his people.

### Exodus 23:25–26

**KJV:** And ye shall serve the LORD your God, and he shall bless thy bread, and thy water; and I will take sickness away from the midst of thee. There shall nothing cast their young, nor be barren, in thy land: the number of thy days I will fulfil.

**NKJV:** So you shall serve the L<small>ORD</small> your God, and He will bless your bread and your water. And I will take sickness away from the midst of you. No one shall suffer miscarriage or be barren in your land; I will fulfill the number of your days.

### Deuteronomy 6:2

**KJV:** That thou mightest fear the L<small>ORD</small> thy God, to keep all his statutes and his commandments, which I command thee, thou, and thy son, and thy son's son, all the days of thy life; and that thy days may be prolonged.

**NKJV:** That you may fear the L<small>ORD</small> your God, to keep all His statutes and His commandments which I command you, you and your son and your grandson, all the days of your life, and that your days may be prolonged.

### Deuteronomy 11:21

**KJV:** That your days may be multiplied, and the days of your children, in the land which the L<small>ORD</small> sware unto your fathers to give them, as the days of heaven upon the earth.

**NKJV:** That your days and the days of your children may be multiplied in the land of which the L<small>ORD</small> swore to your fathers to give them, like the days of the heavens above the earth.

### 1 Kings 3:14

**KJV:** And if thou wilt walk in my ways, to keep my statutes and my commandments, as thy father David did walk, then I will lengthen thy days.

**NKJV:** So if you walk in My ways, to keep My statutes and My commandments, as your father David walked, then I will lengthen your days.

# Long Life

### Psalm 91:16

**KJV:** With long life will I satisfy him, and shew him my salvation.

**NKJV:** With long life I will satisfy him, and show him My salvation.

### Psalm 118:17

**KJV:** I shall not die, but live, and declare the works of the LORD.

**NKJV:** I shall not die, but live, and declare the works of the LORD.

### Proverbs 3:1–2

**KJV:** My son, forget not my law; but let thine heart keep my commandments: for length of days, and long life, and peace, shall they add to thee.

**NKJV:** My son, do not forget my law, but let your heart keep my commands; for length of days and long life and peace they will add to you.

### Proverbs 3:16

**KJV:** Length of days is in her right hand; and in her left hand riches and honour.

**NKJV:** Length of days is in her right hand, in her left hand riches and honor.

### Proverbs 4:10

**KJV:** Hear, O my son, and receive my sayings; and the years of thy life shall be many.

**NKJV:** Hear, my son, and receive my sayings, and the years of your life will be many.

### Proverbs 9:11

**KJV:** For by me thy days shall be multiplied, and the years of thy life shall be increased.

**NKJV:** For by me your days will be multiplied, and years of life will be added to you.

### Proverbs 10:27

**KJV:** The fear of the Lord prolongeth days: but the years of the wicked shall be shortened.

**NKJV:** The fear of the Lord prolongs days, but the years of the wicked will be shortened.

### Proverbs 12:28

**KJV:** In the way of righteousness is life; and in the pathway thereof there is no death.

**NKJV:** In the way of righteousness is life, and in its pathway there is no death.

### Ephesians 6:3

**KJV:** That it may be well with thee, and thou mayest live long on the earth.

**NKJV:** That it may be well with you and you may live long on the earth.

### 1 Peter 3:10

**KJV:** For he that will love life, and see good days, let him refrain his tongue from evil, and his lips that they speak no guile.

**NKJV:** For "He who would love life and see good days, let him refrain his tongue from evil, and his lips from speaking deceit."

# 36

# Love: God's Love for Me

> "Thank You, Father, that You love me as much as You do Jesus."
> John 17:23

### Psalm 86:15

**KJV:** But thou, O Lord, art a God full of compassion, and gracious, longsuffering, and plenteous in mercy and truth.

**NKJV:** But You, O Lord, are a God full of compassion, and gracious, longsuffering and abundant in mercy and truth.

### Jeremiah 31:3

**KJV:** The Lord hath appeared of old unto me, saying, Yea, I have loved thee with an everlasting love: therefore with lovingkindness have I drawn thee.

**NKJV:** The Lord has appeared of old to me, saying: "Yes, I have loved you with an everlasting love; therefore with lovingkindness I have drawn you."

### John 3:16

**KJV:** For God so loved the world, that he gave his only begotten Son, that whosoever believeth in him should not perish, but have everlasting life.

**NKJV:** For God so loved the world that He gave His only begotten Son, that whoever believes in Him should not perish but have everlasting life.

### John 15:13

**KJV:** Greater love hath no man than this, that a man lay down his life for his friends.

**NKJV:** Greater love has no one than this, than to lay down one's life for his friends.

### John 17:23

**KJV:** I in them, and thou in me, that they may be made perfect in one; and that the world may know that thou hast sent me, and hast loved them, as thou hast loved me.

**NKJV:** I in them, and You in Me; that they may be made perfect in one, and that the world may know that You have sent Me, and have loved them as You have loved Me.

### Romans 5:5

**KJV:** And hope maketh not ashamed; because the love of God is shed abroad in our hearts by the Holy Ghost which is given unto us.

**NKJV:** Now hope does not disappoint, because the love of God has been poured out in our hearts by the Holy Spirit who was given to us.

### Romans 5:8

**KJV:** But God commendeth his love toward us, in that, while we were yet sinners, Christ died for us.

**NKJV:** But God demonstrates His own love toward us, in that while we were still sinners, Christ died for us.

### Ephesians 2:4–5

**KJV:** But God, who is rich in mercy, for his great love wherewith he loved us, even when we were dead in sins, hath quickened us together with Christ, (by grace ye are saved).

**NKJV:** But God, who is rich in mercy, because of His great love with which He loved us, even when we were dead in trespasses, made us alive together with Christ (by grace you have been saved).

### Ephesians 3:14–19

**KJV:** For this cause I bow my knees unto the Father of our Lord Jesus Christ, of whom the whole family in heaven and earth is named, that he would grant you, according to the riches of his glory, to be strengthened with might by his Spirit in the inner man; that Christ may dwell in your hearts by faith; that ye, being rooted and grounded in love, may be able to comprehend with all saints what is the breadth, and length, and depth, and height; and to know the love of Christ, which passeth knowledge, that ye might be filled with all the fulness of God.

**NKJV:** For this reason I bow my knees to the Father of our Lord Jesus Christ, from whom the whole family in heaven and earth is named, that He would grant you, according to the riches of His glory, to be strengthened with might through His Spirit in the inner man, that Christ may dwell in your hearts through faith; that you, being rooted and grounded in love, may be able to comprehend with all the saints what is the width and length and depth and height—to know the love of Christ which passes knowledge; that you may be filled with all the fullness of God.

### 1 John 3:1

**KJV:** Behold, what manner of love the Father hath bestowed upon us, that we should be called the sons of God: therefore the world knoweth us not, because it knew him not.

**NKJV:** Behold what manner of love the Father has bestowed on us, that we should be called children of God! Therefore the world does not know us, because it did not know Him.

### 1 John 4:8–10

**KJV:** He that loveth not knoweth not God; for God is love. In this was manifested the love of God toward us, because that God sent his only begotten Son into the world, that we might live through him. Herein is love, not that we loved God, but that he loved us, and sent his Son to be the propitiation for our sins.

**NKJV:** He who does not love does not know God, for God is love. In this the love of God was manifested toward us, that God has sent His only begotten Son into the world, that we might live through Him. In this is love, not that we loved God, but that He loved us and sent His Son to be the propitiation for our sins.

### 1 John 4:16–19

**KJV:** And we have known and believed the love that God hath to us. God is love; and he that dwelleth in love dwelleth in God, and God in him. Herein is our love made perfect, that we may have boldness in the day of judgment: because as he is, so are we in this world. There is no fear in love; but perfect love casteth out fear: because fear hath torment. He that feareth is not made perfect in love. We love him, because he first loved us.

**NKJV:** And we have known and believed the love that God has for us. God is love, and he who abides in love abides in God, and God in him. Love has been perfected among us in this: that we may have boldness in the day of judgment; because as He is, so are we in this world. There is no fear in love; but perfect love casts out fear, because fear involves torment. But he who fears has not been made perfect in love. We love Him because He first loved us.

Pray the Word

# 37
# Love: God's Love Toward Others

> "Thank You, Father, that today I love my enemies, I do good to them, and I pray for them."
> Matthew 5:44

### Proverbs 17:17

**KJV:** A friend loveth at all times, and a brother is born for adversity.

**NKJV:** A friend loves at all times, and a brother is born for adversity.

### Matthew 5:44

**KJV:** But I say unto you, Love your enemies, bless them that curse you, do good to them that hate you, and pray for them which despitefully use you, and persecute you.

**NKJV:** But I say to you, love your enemies, bless those who curse you, do good to those who hate you, and pray for those who spitefully use you and persecute you.

### Mark 12:29–30

**KJV:** And Jesus answered him, The first of all the commandments is, Hear, O Israel; the Lord our God is one Lord: and thou shalt love the Lord thy God with all thy heart, and with all thy soul, and with all thy mind, and with all thy strength: this is the first commandment.

**NKJV:** Jesus answered him, "The first of all the commandments is: 'Hear, O Israel, the Lord our God, the Lord is one. And you shall love the Lord your God with all your heart, with all your soul, with all your mind, and with all your strength.' This is the first commandment."

### Romans 12:9–10

**KJV:** Let love be without dissimulation. Abhor that which is evil; cleave to that which is good. Be kindly affectioned one to another with brotherly love; in honour preferring one another.

**NKJV:** Let love be without hypocrisy. Abhor what is evil. Cling to what is good. Be kindly affectionate to one another with brotherly love, in honor giving preference to one another.

### Romans 13:8

**KJV:** Owe no man any thing, but to love one another: for he that loveth another hath fulfilled the law.

**NKJV:** Owe no one anything except to love one another, for he who loves another has fulfilled the law.

### Romans 13:10

**KJV:** Love worketh no ill to his neighbour: therefore love is the fulfilling of the law.

**NKJV:** Love does no harm to a neighbor; therefore love is the fulfillment of the law.

### 1 Corinthians 13:4–8

**KJV:** Charity suffereth long, and is kind; charity envieth not; charity vaunteth not itself, is not puffed up, doth not behave itself unseemly, seeketh not her own, is not easily provoked, thinketh no evil; rejoiceth not in iniquity, but rejoiceth in the truth; beareth all things, believeth all things, hopeth all things, endureth all things. Charity never faileth: but whether there be prophecies, they shall fail; whether there be tongues, they shall cease; whether there be knowledge, it shall vanish away.

**NKJV:** Love suffers long and is kind; love does not envy; love does not parade itself, is not puffed up; does not behave rudely, does not seek its own, is not provoked, thinks no evil; does not rejoice in iniquity, but rejoices in the truth; bears all things, believes all things, hopes all things, endures all things. Love never fails. But whether there are prophecies, they will fail; whether there are tongues, they will cease; whether there is knowledge, it will vanish away.

### 1 Corinthians 13:13

**KJV:** And now abideth faith, hope, charity, these three; but the greatest of these is charity.

**NKJV:** And now abide faith, hope, love, these three; but the greatest of these is love.

### Colossians 3:14

**KJV:** And above all these things put on charity, which is the bond of perfectness.

**NKJV:** But above all these things put on love, which is the bond of perfection.

### Ephesians 4:32

**KJV:** And be ye kind one to another, tenderhearted, forgiving one another, even as God for Christ's sake hath forgiven you.

**NKJV:** And be kind to one another, tenderhearted, forgiving one another, even as God in Christ forgave you.

### 1 Peter 4:8

**KJV:** And above all things have fervent charity among yourselves: for charity shall cover the multitude of sins.

**NKJV:** And above all things have fervent love for one another, for "love will cover a multitude of sins."

### 1 John 4:11

**KJV:** Beloved, if God so loved us, we ought also to love one another.

**NKJV:** Beloved, if God so loved us, we also ought to love one another.

# 38 Marriage

> "Thank You, Father, that today I am patient and kind with my spouse."
> 1 Corinthians 13:4

### Genesis 1:27–28

**KJV:** So God created man in his own image, in the image of God created he him; male and female created he them. And God blessed them, and God said unto them, Be fruitful, and multiply, and replenish the earth, and subdue it: and have dominion over the fish of the sea, and over the fowl of the air, and over every living thing that moveth upon the earth.

**NKJV:** So God created man in His own image; in the image of God He created him; male and female He created them. Then God blessed them, and God said to them, "Be fruitful and multiply; fill the earth and subdue it; have dominion over the fish of the sea, over the birds of the air, and over every living thing that moves on the earth."

### Proverbs 5:19

**KJV:** Let her be as the loving hind and pleasant roe; let her breasts satisfy thee at all times; and be thou ravished always with her love.

**NKJV:** As a loving deer and a graceful doe, let her breasts satisfy you at all times; and always be enraptured with her love.

### Ecclesiastes 4:9–12

**KJV:** Two are better than one; because they have a good reward for their labour. For if they fall, the one will lift up his fellow: but woe to him that is alone when he falleth; for he hath not another to help him up. Again, if two lie together, then they have heat: but how can one be warm alone? And if one prevail against him, two shall withstand him; and a threefold cord is not quickly broken.

**NKJV:** Two are better than one, because they have a good reward for their labor. For if they fall, one will lift up his companion. But woe to him who is alone when he falls, for he has no one to help him up. Again, if two lie down together, they will keep warm; but how can one be warm alone? Though one may be overpowered by another, two can withstand him. And a threefold cord is not quickly broken.

### Song of Solomon 4:9

**KJV:** Thou hast ravished my heart, my sister, my spouse; thou hast ravished my heart with one of thine eyes, with one chain of thy neck.

**NKJV:** You have ravished my heart, my sister, my spouse; you have ravished my heart with one look of your eyes, with one link of your necklace.

### Mark 10:7–9

**KJV:** For this cause shall a man leave his father and mother, and cleave to his wife; and they twain shall be one flesh: so then they are no more twain, but one flesh. What therefore God hath joined together, let not man put asunder.

**NKJV:** "For this reason a man shall leave his father and mother and be joined to his wife, and the two shall become one flesh"; so then they are no longer two, but one flesh. Therefore what God has joined together, let not man separate.

### 1 Corinthians 13:4–5

**KJV:** Charity suffereth long, and is kind; charity envieth not; charity vaunteth not itself, is not puffed up, doth not behave itself unseemly, seeketh not her own, is not easily provoked, thinketh no evil.

**NKJV:** Love suffers long and is kind; love does not envy; love does not parade itself, is not puffed up; does not behave rudely, does not seek its own, is not provoked, thinks no evil.

### Ephesians 4:32

**KJV:** And be ye kind one to another, tenderhearted, forgiving one another, even as God for Christ's sake hath forgiven you.

**NKJV:** And be kind to one another, tenderhearted, forgiving one another, even as God in Christ forgave you.

### Ephesians 5:25–33

**KJV:** Husbands, love your wives, even as Christ also loved the church, and gave himself for it; that he might sanctify and cleanse it with the washing of water by the word, that he might present it to himself a glorious church, not having spot, or wrinkle, or any such thing; but that it should be holy and without blemish. So ought men to love their wives as their own bodies. He that loveth his wife loveth himself. For no man ever yet hated his own flesh; but nourisheth and cherisheth it, even as the Lord the church: for we are members of his body, of his flesh, and of his bones. For this cause shall a man leave his father and mother, and shall be joined unto his wife, and they two shall be one flesh. This is a great mystery: but I speak concerning Christ and the church. Nevertheless let every one of you in particular so love his wife even as himself; and the wife see that she reverence her husband.

**NKJV:** Husbands, love your wives, just as Christ also loved the church and gave Himself for her, that He might sanctify and cleanse her with the washing of water by the word, that He might present her to Himself a glorious church, not having spot or wrinkle or any such thing, but that she should be holy and without blemish. So husbands ought to love their own wives as their own bodies; he who loves his wife loves himself. For no one ever hated his own flesh, but nourishes and cherishes it, just as the Lord does the church. For we are members of His body, of His flesh and of His bones. "For this reason a man shall leave his father and mother and be joined to his wife, and the two shall become one flesh." This is a great mystery, but I speak concerning Christ and the church. Nevertheless let each one of you in particular so love his own wife as himself, and let the wife see that she respects her husband.

### Colossians 3:13

**KJV:** Forbearing one another, and forgiving one another, if any man have a quarrel against any: even as Christ forgave you, so also do ye.

**NKJV:** Bearing with one another, and forgiving one another, if anyone has a complaint against another; even as Christ forgave you, so you also must do.

### Colossians 3:18–19

**KJV:** Wives, submit yourselves unto your own husbands, as it is fit in the Lord. Husbands, love your wives, and be not bitter against them.

**NKJV:** Wives, submit to your own husbands, as is fitting in the Lord. Husbands, love your wives and do not be bitter toward them.

## Marriage

### 1 Peter 3:1–7

**KJV:** Likewise, ye wives, be in subjection to your own husbands; that, if any obey not the word, they also may without the word be won by the conversation of the wives; while they behold your chaste conversation coupled with fear. Whose adorning let it not be that outward adorning of plaiting the hair, and of wearing of gold, or of putting on of apparel; but let it be the hidden man of the heart, in that which is not corruptible, even the ornament of a meek and quiet spirit, which is in the sight of God of great price. For after this manner in the old time the holy women also, who trusted in God, adorned themselves, being in subjection unto their own husbands: even as Sara obeyed Abraham, calling him lord: whose daughters ye are, as long as ye do well, and are not afraid with any amazement. Likewise, ye husbands, dwell with them according to knowledge, giving honour unto the wife, as unto the weaker vessel, and as being heirs together of the grace of life; that your prayers be not hindered.

**NKJV:** Wives, likewise, be submissive to your own husbands, that even if some do not obey the word, they, without a word, may be won by the conduct of their wives, when they observe your chaste conduct accompanied by fear. Do not let your adornment be merely outward—arranging the hair, wearing gold, or putting on fine apparel—rather let it be the hidden person of the heart, with the incorruptible beauty of a gentle and quiet spirit, which is very precious in the sight of God. For in this manner, in former times, the holy women who trusted in God also adorned themselves, being submissive to their own husbands, as Sarah obeyed Abraham, calling him lord, whose daughters you are if you do good and are not afraid with any terror. Husbands, likewise, dwell with them with understanding, giving honor to the wife, as to the weaker vessel, and as being heirs together of the grace of life, that your prayers may not be hindered.

## Pray the Word

# 39 Negative Thoughts

> "Thank You, Father, that today I cast down imaginations contrary to Your Word and bring every thought into captivity."
> 2 Corinthians 10:5

### Proverbs 3:5

**KJV:** Trust in the Lord with all thine heart; and lean not unto thine own understanding.

**NKJV:** Trust in the Lord with all your heart, and lean not on your own understanding.

### Proverbs 4:23

**KJV:** Keep thy heart with all diligence; for out of it are the issues of life.

**NKJV:** Keep your heart with all diligence, for out of it spring the issues of life.

### Proverbs 8:5–6

**KJV:** O ye simple, understand wisdom: and, ye fools, be ye of an understanding heart. Hear; for I will speak of excellent things; and the opening of my lips shall be right things.

**NKJV:** O you simple ones, understand prudence, and you fools, be of an understanding heart. Listen, for I will speak of excellent things, and from the opening of my lips will come right things.

### Romans 12:2

**KJV:** And be not conformed to this world: but be ye transformed by the renewing of your mind, that ye may prove what is that good, and acceptable, and perfect, will of God.

**NKJV:** And do not be conformed to this world, but be transformed by the renewing of your mind, that you may prove what is that good and acceptable and perfect will of God.

### 2 Corinthians 10:5

**KJV:** Casting down imaginations, and every high thing that exalteth itself against the knowledge of God, and bringing into captivity every thought to the obedience of Christ.

**NKJV:** Casting down arguments and every high thing that exalts itself against the knowledge of God, bringing every thought into captivity to the obedience of Christ.

### Ephesians 4:23

**KJV:** And be renewed in the spirit of your mind.

**NKJV:** And be renewed in the spirit of your mind.

### Philippians 4:8

**KJV:** Finally, brethren, whatsoever things are true, whatsoever things are honest, whatsoever things are just, whatsoever things are pure, whatsoever things are lovely, whatsoever things are of good report; if there be any virtue, and if there be any praise, think on these things.

**NKJV:** Finally, brethren, whatever things are true, whatever things are noble, whatever things are just, whatever things are pure, whatever things are lovely, whatever things are of good report, if there is any virtue and if there is anything praiseworthy—meditate on these things.

### Colossians 3:2

**KJV:** Set your affection on things above, not on things on the earth.

**NKJV:** Set your mind on things above, not on things on the earth.

### 2 Timothy 1:7

**KJV:** For God hath not given us the spirit of fear; but of power, and of love, and of a sound mind.

**NKJV:** For God has not given us a spirit of fear, but of power and of love and of a sound mind.

Pray the Word

# Obedience to God

*"Thank You, Father, that today I deny myself, take up my cross, and follow You."*
Luke 9:23

### Deuteronomy 28:1

**KJV:** And it shall come to pass, if thou shalt hearken diligently unto the voice of the LORD thy God, to observe and to do all his commandments which I command thee this day, that the LORD thy God will set thee on high above all nations of the earth.

**NKJV:** Now it shall come to pass, if you diligently obey the voice of the LORD your God, to observe carefully all His commandments which I command you today, that the LORD your God will set you high above all nations of the earth.

### Joshua 1:8

**KJV:** This book of the law shall not depart out of thy mouth; but thou shalt meditate therein day and night, that thou mayest observe to do according to all that is written therein: for then thou shalt make thy way prosperous, and then thou shalt have good success.

**NKJV:** This Book of the Law shall not depart from your mouth, but you shall meditate in it day and night, that you may observe to do according to all that is written in it. For then you will make your way prosperous, and then you will have good success.

### Psalm 119:60

**KJV:** I made haste, and delayed not to keep thy commandments.

**NKJV:** I made haste, and did not delay to keep Your commandments.

### Proverbs 4:10

**KJV:** Hear, O my son, and receive my sayings; and the years of thy life shall be many.

**NKJV:** Hear, my son, and receive my sayings, and the years of your life will be many.

### Proverbs 6:20

**KJV:** My son, keep thy father's commandment, and forsake not the law of thy mother.

**NKJV:** My son, keep your father's command, and do not forsake the law of your mother.

### Luke 9:23

**KJV:** And he said to them all, If any man will come after me, let him deny himself, and take up his cross daily, and follow me.

**NKJV:** Then He said to them all, "If anyone desires to come after Me, let him deny himself, and take up his cross daily, and follow Me."

### John 14:15

**KJV:** If ye love me, keep my commandments.

**NKJV:** If you love Me, keep My commandments.

### John 14:23

**KJV:** Jesus answered and said unto him, If a man love me, he will keep my words: and my Father will love him, and we will come unto him, and make our abode with him.

**NKJV:** Jesus answered and said to him, "If anyone loves Me, he will keep My word; and My Father will love him, and we will come to him and make our home with him."

### Luke 12:48

**KJV:** For unto whomsoever much is given, of him shall be much required: and to whom men have committed much, of him they will ask the more.

**NKJV:** For everyone to whom much is given, from him much will be required; and to whom much has been committed, of him they will ask the more.

### Romans 5:19

**KJV:** For as by one man's disobedience many were made sinners, so by the obedience of one shall many be made righteous.

**NKJV:** For as by one man's disobedience many were made sinners, so also by one Man's obedience many will be made righteous.

### Romans 12:1

**KJV:** I beseech you therefore, brethren, by the mercies of God, that ye present your bodies a living sacrifice, holy, acceptable unto God, which is your reasonable service.

**NKJV:** I beseech you therefore, brethren, by the mercies of God, that you present your bodies a living sacrifice, holy, acceptable to God, which is your reasonable service.

### Philippians 2:12–13

**KJV:** Wherefore, my beloved, as ye have always obeyed, not as in my presence only, but now much more in my absence, work out your own salvation with fear and trembling. For it is God which worketh in you both to will and to do of his good pleasure.

**NKJV:** Therefore, my beloved, as you have always obeyed, not as in my presence only, but now much more in my absence, work out your own salvation with fear and trembling; for it is God who works in you both to will and to do for His good pleasure.

### James 1:22

**KJV:** But be ye doers of the word, and not hearers only, deceiving your own selves.

**NKJV:** But be doers of the word, and not hearers only, deceiving yourselves.

### James 1:25

**KJV:** But whoso looketh into the perfect law of liberty, and continueth therein, he being not a forgetful hearer, but a doer of the work, this man shall be blessed in his deed.

**NKJV:** But he who looks into the perfect law of liberty and continues in it, and is not a forgetful hearer but a doer of the work, this one will be blessed in what he does.

## Obedience to God

### 1 John 3:21–22

**KJV:** Beloved, if our heart condemn us not, then have we confidence toward God. And whatsoever we ask, we receive of him, because we keep his commandments, and do those things that are pleasing in his sight.

**NKJV:** Beloved, if our heart does not condemn us, we have confidence toward God. And whatever we ask we receive from Him, because we keep His commandments and do those things that are pleasing in His sight.

Pray the Word

# 41

## Overcoming My Past

> "Thank You, Father, that today I forget those things which are behind and press toward the mark of the high calling in Christ."
> Philippians 3:13–14

### Proverbs 28:13

**KJV:** He that covereth his sins shall not prosper: but whoso confesseth and forsaketh them shall have mercy.

**NKJV:** He who covers his sins will not prosper, but whoever confesses and forsakes them will have mercy.

### Isaiah 43:18–19

**KJV:** Remember ye not the former things, neither consider the things of old. Behold, I will do a new thing; now it shall spring forth; shall ye not know it? I will even make a way in the wilderness, and rivers in the desert.

**NKJV:** Do not remember the former things, nor consider the things of old. Behold, I will do a new thing, now it shall spring forth; shall you not know it? I will even make a road in the wilderness and rivers in the desert.

### Isaiah 43:25

**KJV:** I, even I, am he that blotteth out thy transgressions for mine own sake, and will not remember thy sins.

**NKJV:** I, even I, am He who blots out your transgressions for My own sake; and I will not remember your sins.

### Luke 9:62

**KJV:** And Jesus said unto him, no man, having put his hand to the plough, and looking back, is fit for the kingdom of God.

**NKJV:** But Jesus said to him, "No one, having put his hand to the plow, and looking back, is fit for the kingdom of God."

### Romans 8:1

**KJV:** There is therefore now no condemnation to them which are in Christ Jesus, who walk not after the flesh, but after the Spirit.

**NKJV:** There is therefore now no condemnation to those who are in Christ Jesus, who do not walk according to the flesh, but according to the Spirit.

### Philippians 3:13–14

**KJV:** Brethren, I count not myself to have apprehended: but this one thing I do, forgetting those things which are behind, and reaching forth unto those things which are before, I press toward the mark for the prize of the high calling of God in Christ Jesus.

**NKJV:** Brethren, I do not count myself to have apprehended; but one thing I do, forgetting those things which are behind and reaching forward to those things which are ahead, I press toward the goal for the prize of the upward call of God in Christ Jesus.

### 2 Corinthians 5:17–18

**KJV:** Therefore if any man be in Christ, he is a new creature: old things are passed away; behold, all things are become new. And all things are of God, who hath reconciled us to himself by Jesus Christ, and hath given to us the ministry of reconciliation.

**NKJV:** Therefore, if anyone is in Christ, he is a new creation; old things have passed away; behold, all things have become new. Now all things are of God, who has reconciled us to Himself through Jesus Christ, and has given us the ministry of reconciliation.

### Hebrews 8:12

**KJV:** For I will be merciful to their unrighteousness, and their sins and their iniquities will I remember no more.

**NKJV:** For I will be merciful to their unrighteousness, and their sins and their lawless deeds I will remember no more.

### Hebrews 11:15

**KJV:** And truly, if they had been mindful of that country from whence they came out, they might have had opportunity to have returned.

**NKJV:** And truly if they had called to mind that country from which they had come out, they would have had opportunity to return.

### 1 John 1:9

**KJV:** If we confess our sins, he is faithful and just to forgive us our sins, and to cleanse us from all unrighteousness.

**NKJV:** If we confess our sins, He is faithful and just to forgive us our sins and to cleanse us from all unrighteousness.

Pray the Word

# 42 Power of Our Words

> "Thank You, Father, that today I keep my tongue from evil and my lips from speaking guile."
> Psalm 34:13

### Psalm 34:13

**KJV:** Keep thy tongue from evil, and thy lips from speaking guile.

**NKJV:** Keep your tongue from evil, and your lips from speaking deceit.

### Psalm 141:3

**KJV:** Set a watch, O Lord, before my mouth; keep the door of my lips.

**NKJV:** Set a guard, O Lord, over my mouth; keep watch over the door of my lips.

### Proverbs 10:19

**KJV:** In the multitude of words there wanteth not sin: but he that refraineth his lips is wise.

**NKJV:** In the multitude of words sin is not lacking, but he who restrains his lips is wise.

### Proverbs 12:18–19

**KJV:** There is that speaketh like the piercings of a sword: but the tongue of the wise is health. The lip of truth shall be established for ever: but a lying tongue is but for a moment.

**NKJV:** There is one who speaks like the piercings of a sword, but the tongue of the wise promotes health. The truthful lip shall be established forever, but a lying tongue is but for a moment.

### Proverbs 15:1

**KJV:** A soft answer turneth away wrath: but grievous words stir up anger.

**NKJV:** A soft answer turns away wrath, but a harsh word stirs up anger.

### Proverbs 15:4

**KJV:** A wholesome tongue is a tree of life: but perverseness therein is a breach in the spirit.

**NKJV:** A wholesome tongue is a tree of life, but perverseness in it breaks the spirit.

### Proverbs 15:28

**KJV:** The heart of the righteous studieth to answer: but the mouth of the wicked poureth out evil things.

**NKJV:** The heart of the righteous studies how to answer, but the mouth of the wicked pours forth evil.

### Proverbs 16:24

**KJV:** Pleasant words are as an honeycomb, sweet to the soul, and health to the bones.

**NKJV:** Pleasant words are like a honeycomb, sweetness to the soul and health to the bones.

### Proverbs 16:28

**KJV:** A froward man soweth strife: and a whisperer separateth chief friends.

**NKJV:** A perverse man sows strife, and a whisperer separates the best of friends.

### Proverbs 17:9

**KJV:** He that covereth a transgression seeketh love; but he that repeateth a matter separateth very friends.

**NKJV:** He who covers a transgression seeks love, but he who repeats a matter separates friends.

### Proverbs 17:27–28

**KJV:** He that hath knowledge spareth his words: and a man of understanding is of an excellent spirit. Even a fool, when he holdeth his peace, is counted wise: and he that shutteth his lips is esteemed a man of understanding.

**NKJV:** He who has knowledge spares his words, and a man of understanding is of a calm spirit. Even a fool is counted wise when he holds his peace; when he shuts his lips, he is considered perceptive.

### Proverbs 18:8

**KJV:** The words of a talebearer are as wounds, and they go down into the innermost parts of the belly.

**NKJV:** The words of a talebearer are like tasty trifles, and they go down into the inmost body.

### Proverbs 18:20–21

**KJV:** A man's belly shall be satisfied with the fruit of his mouth; and with the increase of his lips shall he be filled. Death and life are in the power of the tongue: and they that love it shall eat the fruit thereof.

**NKJV:** A man's stomach shall be satisfied from the fruit of his mouth; from the produce of his lips he shall be filled. Death and life are in the power of the tongue, and those who love it will eat its fruit.

### Proverbs 21:23

**KJV:** Whoso keepeth his mouth and his tongue keepeth his soul from troubles.

**NKJV:** Whoever guards his mouth and tongue keeps his soul from troubles.

### Proverbs 26:20

**KJV:** Where no wood is, there the fire goeth out: so where there is no talebearer, the strife ceaseth.

**NKJV:** Where there is no wood, the fire goes out; and where there is no talebearer, strife ceases.

### Proverbs 29:20

**KJV:** Seest thou a man that is hasty in his words? There is more hope of a fool than of him.

**NKJV:** Do you see a man hasty in his words? There is more hope for a fool than for him.

### Matthew 15:11

**KJV:** Not that which goeth into the mouth defileth a man; but that which cometh out of the mouth, this defileth a man.

**NKJV:** Not what goes into the mouth defiles a man; but what comes out of the mouth, this defiles a man.

### Mark 11:23

**KJV:** For verily I say unto you, that whosoever shall say unto this mountain, be thou removed, and be thou cast into the sea; and shall not doubt in his heart, but shall believe that those things which he saith shall come to pass; he shall have whatsoever he saith.

**NKJV:** For assuredly, I say to you, whoever says to this mountain, "Be removed and be cast into the sea," and does not doubt in his heart, but believes that those things he says will be done, he will have whatever he says.

### Ephesians 4:29

**KJV:** Let no corrupt communication proceed out of your mouth, but that which is good to the use of edifying, that it may minister grace unto the hearers.

**NKJV:** Let no corrupt word proceed out of your mouth, but what is good for necessary edification, that it may impart grace to the hearers.

### James 1:19

**KJV:** Wherefore, my beloved brethren, let every man be swift to hear, slow to speak, slow to wrath.

**NKJV:** So then, my beloved brethren, let every man be swift to hear, slow to speak, slow to wrath.

### James 3:3–6

**KJV:** Behold, we put bits in the horses' mouths, that they may obey us; and we turn about their whole body. Behold also the ships, which though they be so great, and are driven of fierce winds, yet are they turned about with a very small helm, whithersoever the governor listeth. Even so the tongue is a little member, and boasteth great things. Behold, how great a matter a little fire kindleth! And the tongue is a fire, a world of iniquity: so is the tongue among our members, that it defileth the whole body, and setteth on fire the course of nature; and it is set on fire of hell.

**NKJV:** Indeed, we put bits in horses' mouths that they may obey us, and we turn their whole body. Look also at ships: although they are so large and are driven by fierce winds, they are turned by a very small rudder wherever the pilot desires. Even so the tongue is a little member and boasts great things. See how great a forest a little fire kindles! And the tongue is a fire, a world of iniquity. The tongue is so set among our members that it defiles the whole body, and sets on fire the course of nature; and it is set on fire by hell.

### James 3:10

**KJV:** Out of the same mouth proceedeth blessing and cursing. My brethren, these things ought not so to be.

**NKJV:** Out of the same mouth proceed blessing and cursing. My brethren, these things ought not to be so.

### 1 Peter 3:10

**KJV:** For he that will love life, and see good days, let him refrain his tongue from evil, and his lips that they speak no guile.

**NKJV:** For "He who would love life and see good days, let him refrain his tongue from evil, and his lips from speaking deceit."

# Pray the Word

# 43 Prayer

> "Thank You, Father, that the effectual, fervent prayer of a righteous man avails much."
> James 5:16

### 2 Chronicles 7:14

**KJV:** If my people, which are called by my name, shall humble themselves, and pray, and seek my face, and turn from their wicked ways; then will I hear from heaven, and will forgive their sin, and will heal their land.

**NKJV:** If My people who are called by My name will humble themselves, and pray and seek My face, and turn from their wicked ways, then I will hear from heaven, and will forgive their sin and heal their land.

### Psalm 145:18

**KJV:** The Lord is nigh unto all them that call upon him, to all that call upon him in truth.

**NKJV:** The Lord is near to all who call upon Him, to all who call upon Him in truth.

### Proverbs 15:8

**KJV:** The sacrifice of the wicked is an abomination to the Lord: but the prayer of the upright is his delight.

**NKJV:** The sacrifice of the wicked is an abomination to the Lord, but the prayer of the upright is His delight.

### Matthew 5:44

**KJV:** But I say unto you, love your enemies, bless them that curse you, do good to them that hate you, and pray for them which despitefully use you, and persecute you.

**NKJV:** But I say to you, love your enemies, bless those who curse you, do good to those who hate you, and pray for those who spitefully use you and persecute you.

### Matthew 6:7

**KJV:** But when ye pray, use not vain repetitions, as the heathen do: for they think that they shall be heard for their much speaking.

**NKJV:** And when you pray, do not use vain repetitions as the heathen do. For they think that they will be heard for their many words.

### Matthew 7:11

**KJV:** If ye then, being evil, know how to give good gifts unto your children, how much more shall your Father which is in heaven give good things to them that ask him?

**NKJV:** If you then, being evil, know how to give good gifts to your children, how much more will your Father who is in heaven give good things to those who ask Him!

### Matthew 26:41

**KJV:** Watch and pray, that ye enter not into temptation: the spirit indeed is willing, but the flesh is weak.

**NKJV:** Watch and pray, lest you enter into temptation. The spirit indeed is willing, but the flesh is weak.

### Mark 11:24

**KJV:** Therefore I say unto you, what things soever ye desire, when ye pray, believe that ye receive them, and ye shall have them.

**NKJV:** Therefore I say to you, whatever things you ask when you pray, believe that you receive them, and you will have them.

### Luke 18:1

**KJV:** And he spake a parable unto them to this end, that men ought always to pray, and not to faint.

**NKJV:** Then He spoke a parable to them, that men always ought to pray and not lose heart.

### John 16:23–24

**KJV:** And in that day ye shall ask me nothing. Verily, verily, I say unto you, Whatsoever ye shall ask the Father in my name, he will give it you. Hitherto have ye asked nothing in my name: ask, and ye shall receive, that your joy may be full.

**NKJV:** And in that day you will ask Me nothing. Most assuredly, I say to you, whatever you ask the Father in My name He will give you. Until now you have asked nothing in My name. Ask, and you will receive, that your joy may be full.

### Romans 8:26–27

**KJV:** Likewise the Spirit also helpeth our infirmities: for we know not what we should pray for as we ought: but the Spirit itself maketh intercession for us with groanings which cannot be uttered. And he that searcheth the hearts knoweth what is the mind of the Spirit, because he maketh intercession for the saints according to the will of God.

**NKJV:** Likewise the Spirit also helps in our weaknesses. For we do not know what we should pray for as we ought, but the Spirit Himself makes intercession for us with groanings which cannot be uttered. He who searches the hearts knows what the mind of the Spirit is, because He makes intercession for the saints according to the will of God.

### Romans 12:12

**KJV:** Rejoicing in hope; patient in tribulation; continuing instant in prayer.

**NKJV:** Rejoicing in hope, patient in tribulation, continuing steadfastly in prayer.

### Ephesians 1:16–17

**KJV:** Cease not to give thanks for you, making mention of you in my prayers; that the God of our Lord Jesus Christ, the Father of glory, may give unto you the spirit of wisdom and revelation in the knowledge of him.

**NKJV:** Do not cease to give thanks for you, making mention of you in my prayers: that the God of our Lord Jesus Christ, the Father of glory, may give to you the spirit of wisdom and revelation in the knowledge of Him.

### Ephesians 3:14–20

**KJV:** For this cause I bow my knees unto the Father of our Lord Jesus Christ, of whom the whole family in heaven and earth is named, that he would grant you, according to the riches of his glory, to be strengthened with might by his Spirit in the inner man; that Christ may dwell in your hearts by faith; that ye, being rooted and grounded in love, may be able to comprehend with all saints what is the breadth, and length, and depth, and height; and to know the love of Christ, which passeth knowledge, that ye might be filled with all the fulness of God. Now unto him that is able to do exceeding abundantly above all that we ask or think, according to the power that worketh in us.

**NKJV:** For this reason I bow my knees to the Father of our Lord Jesus Christ, from whom the whole family in heaven and earth is named, that He would grant you, according to the riches of His glory, to be strengthened with might through His Spirit in the inner man, that Christ may dwell in your hearts through faith; that you, being rooted and grounded in love, may be able to comprehend with all the saints what is the width and length and depth and height—to know the love of Christ which passes knowledge; that you may be filled with all the fullness of God. Now to Him who is able to do exceedingly abundantly above all that we ask or think, according to the power that works in us.

### Philippians 1:9–11

**KJV:** And this I pray, that your love may abound yet more and more in knowledge and in all judgment; that ye may approve things that are excellent; that ye may be sincere and without offence till the day of Christ; being filled with the fruits of righteousness, which are by Jesus Christ, unto the glory and praise of God.

**NKJV:** And this I pray, that your love may abound still more and more in knowledge and all discernment, that you may approve the things that are excellent, that you may be sincere and without offense till the day of Christ, being filled with the fruits of righteousness which are by Jesus Christ, to the glory and praise of God.

## Pray the Word

### Philippians 4:6–7

**KJV:** Be careful for nothing; but in every thing by prayer and supplication with thanksgiving let your requests be made known unto God. And the peace of God, which passeth all understanding, shall keep your hearts and minds through Christ Jesus.

**NKJV:** Be anxious for nothing, but in everything by prayer and supplication, with thanksgiving, let your requests be made known to God; and the peace of God, which surpasses all understanding, will guard your hearts and minds through Christ Jesus.

### Colossians 1:9–11

**KJV:** For this cause we also, since the day we heard it, do not cease to pray for you, and to desire that ye might be filled with the knowledge of his will in all wisdom and spiritual understanding; that ye might walk worthy of the Lord unto all pleasing, being fruitful in every good work, and increasing in the knowledge of God; strengthened with all might, according to his glorious power, unto all patience and longsuffering with joyfulness.

**NKJV:** For this reason we also, since the day we heard it, do not cease to pray for you, and to ask that you may be filled with the knowledge of His will in all wisdom and spiritual understanding; that you may walk worthy of the Lord, fully pleasing Him, being fruitful in every good work and increasing in the knowledge of God; strengthened with all might, according to His glorious power, for all patience and longsuffering with joy.

### Colossians 4:2

**KJV:** Continue in prayer, and watch in the same with thanksgiving.

**NKJV:** Continue earnestly in prayer, being vigilant in it with thanksgiving.

### 1 Timothy 2:1–2

**KJV:** I exhort therefore, that, first of all, supplications, prayers, intercessions, and giving of thanks, be made for all men; for kings, and for all that are in authority; that we may lead a quiet and peaceable life in all godliness and honesty.

**NKJV:** Therefore I exhort first of all that supplications, prayers, intercessions, and giving of thanks be made for all men, for kings and all who are in authority, that we may lead a quiet and peaceable life in all godliness and reverence.

### 1 Timothy 2:8

**KJV:** I will therefore that men pray every where, lifting up holy hands, without wrath and doubting.

**NKJV:** I desire therefore that the men pray everywhere, lifting up holy hands, without wrath and doubting.

### James 4:3

**KJV:** Ye ask, and receive not, because ye ask amiss, that ye may consume it upon your lusts.

**NKJV:** You ask and do not receive, because you ask amiss, that you may spend it on your pleasures.

### James 5:13

**KJV:** Is any among you afflicted? Let him pray. Is any merry? Let him sing psalms.

**NKJV:** Is anyone among you suffering? Let him pray. Is anyone cheerful? Let him sing psalms.

### James 5:16

**KJV:** Confess your faults one to another, and pray one for another, that ye may be healed. The effectual fervent prayer of a righteous man availeth much.

**NKJV:** Confess your trespasses to one another, and pray for one another, that you may be healed. The effective, fervent prayer of a righteous man avails much.

### 1 John 5:14–15

**KJV:** And this is the confidence that we have in him, that, if we ask any thing according to his will, he heareth us: and if we know that he hear us, whatsoever we ask, we know that we have the petitions that we desired of him.

**NKJV:** Now this is the confidence that we have in Him, that if we ask anything according to His will, He hears us. And if we know that He hears us, whatever we ask, we know that we have the petitions that we have asked of Him.

# Praying for Those in Authority

> "Thank You, Father, that those in authority nationally, regionally, and locally are the righteous, and therefore the people rejoice."
> Proverbs 29:2

### 2 Chronicles 7:14

**KJV:** If my people, which are called by my name, shall humble themselves, and pray, and seek my face, and turn from their wicked ways; then will I hear from heaven, and will forgive their sin, and will heal their land.

**NKJV:** If My people who are called by My name will humble themselves, and pray and seek My face, and turn from their wicked ways, then I will hear from heaven, and will forgive their sin and heal their land.

### Proverbs 21:1

**KJV:** The king's heart is in the hand of the Lord, as the rivers of water: he turneth it whithersoever he will.

**NKJV:** The king's heart is in the hand of the Lord, like the rivers of water; He turns it wherever He wishes.

### Proverbs 29:2

**KJV:** When the righteous are in authority, the people rejoice: but when the wicked beareth rule, the people mourn.

**NKJV:** When the righteous are in authority, the people rejoice; but when a wicked man rules, the people groan.

### Jeremiah 29:7

**KJV:** And seek the peace of the city whither I have caused you to be carried away captives, and pray unto the Lord for it: for in the peace thereof shall ye have peace.

**NKJV:** And seek the peace of the city where I have caused you to be carried away captive, and pray to the Lord for it; for in its peace you will have peace.

### Romans 13:1

**KJV:** Let every soul be subject unto the higher powers. For there is no power but of God: the powers that be are ordained of God.

**NKJV:** Let every soul be subject to the governing authorities. For there is no authority except from God, and the authorities that exist are appointed by God.

### 1 Timothy 2:1–2

**KJV:** I exhort therefore, that, first of all, supplications, prayers, intercessions, and giving of thanks, be made for all men; for kings, and for all that are in authority; that we may lead a quiet and peaceable life in all godliness and honesty.

**NKJV:** Therefore I exhort first of all that supplications, prayers, intercessions, and giving of thanks be made for all men, for kings and all who are in authority, that we may lead a quiet and peaceable life in all godliness and reverence.

### 1 Peter 2:17

**KJV:** Honour all men. Love the brotherhood. Fear God. Honour the king.

**NKJV:** Honor all people. Love the brotherhood. Fear God. Honor the king.

Pray the Word

# 45 Pregnancy

> "Thank You, Father, that I am a joyful mother of children."
> Psalm 113:9

### Genesis 22:17a
**KJV:** That in blessing I will bless thee, and in multiplying I will multiply thy seed as the stars of the heaven, and as the sand which is upon the sea shore.

**NKJV:** Blessing I will bless you, and multiplying I will multiply your descendants as the stars of the heaven and as the sand which is on the seashore.

### Exodus 23:25–26
**KJV:** And ye shall serve the LORD your God, and he shall bless thy bread, and thy water; and I will take sickness away from the midst of thee. There shall nothing cast their young, nor be barren, in thy land: the number of thy days I will fulfil.

**NKJV:** So you shall serve the Lord your God, and He will bless your bread and your water. And I will take sickness away from the midst of you. No one shall suffer miscarriage or be barren in your land; I will fulfill the number of your days.

### Deuteronomy 7:13

**KJV:** And he will love thee, and bless thee, and multiply thee: he will also bless the fruit of thy womb, and the fruit of thy land, thy corn, and thy wine, and thine oil, the increase of thy kine, and the flocks of thy sheep, in the land which he sware unto thy fathers to give thee.

**NKJV:** And He will love you and bless you and multiply you; He will also bless the fruit of your womb and the fruit of your land, your grain and your new wine and your oil, the increase of your cattle and the offspring of your flock, in the land of which He swore to your fathers to give you.

### Deuteronomy 28:4

**KJV:** Blessed shall be the fruit of thy body, and the fruit of thy ground, and the fruit of thy cattle, the increase of thy kine, and the flocks of thy sheep.

**NKJV:** Blessed shall be the fruit of your body, the produce of your ground and the increase of your herds, the increase of your cattle and the offspring of your flocks.

### Deuteronomy 28:11

**KJV:** And the Lord shall make thee plenteous in goods, in the fruit of thy body, and in the fruit of thy cattle, and in the fruit of thy ground, in the land which the Lord sware unto thy fathers to give thee.

**NKJV:** And the Lord will grant you plenty of goods, in the fruit of your body, in the increase of your livestock, and in the produce of your ground, in the land of which the Lord swore to your fathers to give you.

## Pregnancy

### Psalm 112:2

**KJV:** His seed shall be mighty upon earth: the generation of the upright shall be blessed.

**NKJV:** His descendants will be mighty on earth; the generation of the upright will be blessed.

### Psalm 113:9

**KJV:** He maketh the barren woman to keep house, and to be a joyful mother of children. Praise ye the Lord.

**NKJV:** He grants the barren woman a home, like a joyful mother of children. Praise the Lord!

### Psalm 127:3–5

**KJV:** Lo, children are an heritage of the Lord: and the fruit of the womb is his reward. As arrows are in the hand of a mighty man; so are children of the youth. Happy is the man that hath his quiver full of them: they shall not be ashamed, but they shall speak with the enemies in the gate.

**NKJV:** Behold, children are a heritage from the Lord, the fruit of the womb is a reward. Like arrows in the hand of a warrior, so are the children of one's youth. Happy is the man who has his quiver full of them; they shall not be ashamed, but shall speak with their enemies in the gate.

### Psalm 139:13–16

**KJV:** For thou hast possessed my reins: thou hast covered me in my mother's womb. I will praise thee; for I am fearfully and wonderfully made: marvellous are thy works; and that my soul knoweth right well. My substance was not hid from thee, when I was made in secret, and curiously wrought in the lowest parts of the earth. Thine eyes did see my substance, yet being unperfect; and in thy book all my members were written, which in continuance were fashioned, when as yet there was none of them.

**NKJV:** For You formed my inward parts; You covered me in my mother's womb. I will praise You, for I am fearfully and wonderfully made; marvelous are Your works, and that my soul knows very well. My frame was not hidden from You, when I was made in secret, and skillfully wrought in the lowest parts of the earth. Your eyes saw my substance, being yet unformed. And in Your book they all were written, the days fashioned for me, When as yet there were none of them.

### Isaiah 44:3

**KJV:** For I will pour water upon him that is thirsty, and floods upon the dry ground: I will pour my spirit upon thy seed, and my blessing upon thine offspring.

**NKJV:** For I will pour water on him who is thirsty, and floods on the dry ground; I will pour My Spirit on your descendants, and My blessing on your offspring.

### Isaiah 49:1–2

**KJV:** Listen, O isles, unto me; and hearken, ye people, from far; the LORD hath called me from the womb; from the bowels of my mother hath he made mention of my name. And he hath made my mouth like a sharp sword; in the shadow of his hand hath he hid me, and made me a polished shaft; in his quiver hath he hid me.

**NKJV:** Listen, O coastlands, to Me, and take heed, you peoples from afar! The LORD has called Me from the womb; from the matrix of My mother He has made mention of My name. And He has made My mouth like a sharp sword; in the shadow of His hand He has hidden Me, and made Me a polished shaft; in His quiver He has hidden Me.

## Isaiah 65:23

**KJV:** They shall not labour in vain, nor bring forth for trouble; for they are the seed of the blessed of the Lord, and their offspring with them.

**NKJV:** They shall not labor in vain, nor bring forth children for trouble; for they shall be the descendants of the blessed of the Lord, and their offspring with them.

## Malachi 3:11

**KJV:** And I will rebuke the devourer for your sakes, and he shall not destroy the fruits of your ground; neither shall your vine cast her fruit before the time in the field, saith the Lord of hosts.

**NKJV:** "And I will rebuke the devourer for your sakes, so that he will not destroy the fruit of your ground, nor shall the vine fail to bear fruit for you in the field," says the Lord of hosts.

## Luke 1:37

**KJV:** For with God nothing shall be impossible.

**NKJV:** For with God nothing will be impossible.

## Hebrews 11:11

**KJV:** Through faith also Sara herself received strength to conceive seed, and was delivered of a child when she was past age, because she judged him faithful who had promised.

**NKJV:** By faith Sarah herself also received strength to conceive seed, and she bore a child when she was past the age, because she judged Him faithful who had promised.

# Pray the Word

# Pride
# Humility

> "Thank You, Father, that today I humble myself, and You exalt me in due time."
> 1 Peter 5:6

### 1 Samuel 15:17

**KJV:** And Samuel said, when thou wast little in thine own sight, wast thou not made the head of the tribes of Israel, and the LORD anointed thee king over Israel?

**NKJV:** So Samuel said, "When you were little in your own eyes, were you not head of the tribes of Israel? And did not the LORD anoint you king over Israel?"

### 2 Chronicles 7:14

**KJV:** If my people, which are called by my name, shall humble themselves, and pray, and seek my face, and turn from their wicked ways; then will I hear from heaven, and will forgive their sin, and will heal their land.

**NKJV:** If My people who are called by My name will humble themselves, and pray and seek My face, and turn from their wicked ways, then I will hear from heaven, and will forgive their sin and heal their land.

### Proverbs 11:2

**KJV:** When pride cometh, then cometh shame: but with the lowly is wisdom.

**NKJV:** When pride comes, then comes shame; but with the humble is wisdom.

### Proverbs 12:15

**KJV:** The way of a fool is right in his own eyes: but he that hearkeneth unto counsel is wise.

**NKJV:** The way of a fool is right in his own eyes, but he who heeds counsel is wise.

### Proverbs 13:10

**KJV:** Only by pride cometh contention: but with the well advised is wisdom.

**NKJV:** By pride comes nothing but strife, but with the well-advised is wisdom.

### Proverbs 15:33

**KJV:** The fear of the Lord is the instruction of wisdom; and before honour is humility.

**NKJV:** The fear of the Lord is the instruction of wisdom, and before honor is humility.

## Pride | Humility

### Proverbs 16:5

**KJV:** Every one that is proud in heart is an abomination to the LORD: though hand join in hand, he shall not be unpunished.

**NKJV:** Everyone proud in heart is an abomination to the LORD; though they join forces, none will go unpunished.

### Proverbs 18:12

**KJV:** Before destruction the heart of man is haughty, and before honour is humility.

**NKJV:** Before destruction the heart of a man is haughty, and before honor is humility.

### Proverbs 21:24

**KJV:** Proud and haughty scorner is his name, who dealeth in proud wrath.

**NKJV:** A proud and haughty man—"Scoffer" is his name; he acts with arrogant pride.

### Proverbs 22:4

**KJV:** By humility and the fear of the LORD are riches, and honour, and life.

**NKJV:** By humility and the fear of the LORD are riches and honor and life.

### Proverbs 26:12

**KJV:** Seest thou a man wise in his own conceit? There is more hope of a fool than of him.

**NKJV:** Do you see a man wise in his own eyes? There is more hope for a fool than for him.

# Pray the Word

### Proverbs 27:2

**KJV:** Let another man praise thee, and not thine own mouth; a stranger, and not thine own lips.

**NKJV:** Let another man praise you, and not your own mouth; a stranger, and not your own lips.

### Proverbs 29:23

**KJV:** A man's pride shall bring him low: but honour shall uphold the humble in spirit.

**NKJV:** A man's pride will bring him low, but the humble in spirit will retain honor.

### Micah 6:8

**KJV:** He hath shewed thee, O man, what is good; and what doth the Lord require of thee, but to do justly, and to love mercy, and to walk humbly with thy God?

**NKJV:** He has shown you, O man, what is good; and what does the Lord require of you but to do justly, to love mercy, and to walk humbly with your God?

### Mark 10:43–45

**KJV:** But so shall it not be among you: but whosoever will be great among you, shall be your minister: and whosoever of you will be the chiefest, shall be servant of all. For even the Son of man came not to be ministered unto, but to minister, and to give his life a ransom for many.

**NKJV:** Yet it shall not be so among you; but whoever desires to become great among you shall be your servant. And whoever of you desires to be first shall be slave of all. For even the Son of Man did not come to be served, but to serve, and to give His life a ransom for many.

### Luke 14:11

**KJV:** For whosoever exalteth himself shall be abased; and he that humbleth himself shall be exalted.

**NKJV:** For whoever exalts himself will be humbled, and he who humbles himself will be exalted.

### John 15:5

**KJV:** I am the vine, ye are the branches: he that abideth in me, and I in him, the same bringeth forth much fruit: for without me ye can do nothing.

**NKJV:** I am the vine, you are the branches. He who abides in Me, and I in him, bears much fruit; for without Me you can do nothing.

### Romans 12:3

**KJV:** For I say, through the grace given unto me, to every man that is among you, not to think of himself more highly than he ought to think; but to think soberly, according as God hath dealt to every man the measure of faith.

**NKJV:** For I say, through the grace given to me, to everyone who is among you, not to think of himself more highly than he ought to think, but to think soberly, as God has dealt to each one a measure of faith.

### Ephesians 4:2

**KJV:** With all lowliness and meekness, with longsuffering, forbearing one another in love.

**NKJV:** With all lowliness and gentleness, with longsuffering, bearing with one another in love.

## Pray the Word

### Philippians 2:3–4

**KJV:** Let nothing be done through strife or vainglory; but in lowliness of mind let each esteem other better than themselves. Look not every man on his own things, but every man also on the things of others.

**NKJV:** Let nothing be done through selfish ambition or conceit, but in lowliness of mind let each esteem others better than himself. Let each of you look out not only for his own interests, but also for the interests of others.

### Philippians 2:8

**KJV:** And being found in fashion as a man, he humbled himself, and became obedient unto death, even the death of the cross.

**NKJV:** And being found in appearance as a man, He humbled Himself and became obedient to the point of death, even the death of the cross.

### Colossians 3:12

**KJV:** Put on therefore, as the elect of God, holy and beloved, bowels of mercies, kindness, humbleness of mind, meekness, longsuffering.

**NKJV:** Therefore, as the elect of God, holy and beloved, put on tender mercies, kindness, humility, meekness, longsuffering.

### 1 Peter 5:6

**KJV:** Humble yourselves therefore under the mighty hand of God, that he may exalt you in due time.

**NKJV:** Therefore humble yourselves under the mighty hand of God, that He may exalt you in due time.

### James 4:6

**KJV:** But he giveth more grace. Wherefore he saith, God resisteth the proud, but giveth grace unto the humble.

# 47

## Protection Safety

> "Thank You, Father, that today no evil shall befall me."
> Psalm 91:10

### Psalm 3:3

**KJV:** But thou, O Lord, art a shield for me; my glory, and the lifter up of mine head.

**NKJV:** But You, O Lord, are a shield for me, my glory and the One who lifts up my head.

### Psalm 4:8

**KJV:** I will both lay me down in peace, and sleep: for thou, Lord, only makest me dwell in safety.

**NKJV:** I will both lie down in peace, and sleep; For You alone, O Lord, make me dwell in safety.

### Psalm 32:7

**KJV:** Thou art my hiding place; thou shalt preserve me from trouble; thou shalt compass me about with songs of deliverance.

**NKJV:** You are my hiding place; You shall preserve me from trouble; You shall surround me with songs of deliverance.

### Psalm 37:7

**KJV:** Rest in the Lord, and wait patiently for him: fret not thyself because of him who prospereth in his way, because of the man who bringeth wicked devices to pass.

**NKJV:** Rest in the Lord, and wait patiently for Him; do not fret because of him who prospers in his way, because of the man who brings wicked schemes to pass.

### Psalm 46:1

**KJV:** God is our refuge and strength, a very present help in trouble.

**NKJV:** God is our refuge and strength, a very present help in trouble.

### Psalm 59:16

**KJV:** But I will sing of thy power; yea, I will sing aloud of thy mercy in the morning: for thou hast been my defence and refuge in the day of my trouble.

**NKJV:** But I will sing of Your power; yes, I will sing aloud of your mercy in the morning; for You have been my defense and refuge in the day of my trouble.

### Psalm 91:10

**KJV:** There shall no evil befall thee, neither shall any plague come nigh thy dwelling.

**NKJV:** But He gives more grace. Therefore He says: "God resists the proud, but gives grace to the humble."

### James 4:10

**KJV:** Humble yourselves in the sight of the Lord, and he shall lift you up.

**NKJV:** Humble yourselves in the sight of the Lord, and He will lift you up.

# Pray the Word

**NKJV:** No evil shall befall you, nor shall any plague come near your dwelling.

### Psalm 91:4

**KJV:** He shall cover thee with his feathers, and under his wings shalt thou trust: His truth shall be thy shield and buckler.

**NKJV:** He shall cover you with His feathers, and under His wings you shall take refuge; His truth shall be your shield and buckler.

### Psalm 118:6

**KJV:** The LORD is on my side; I will not fear: what can man do unto me?

**NKJV:** The LORD is on my side; I will not fear. What can man do to me?

### Psalm 118:8

**KJV:** It is better to trust in the LORD than to put confidence in man.

**NKJV:** It is better to trust in the LORD than to put confidence in man.

### Psalm 121:7–8

**KJV:** The LORD shall preserve thee from all evil: he shall preserve thy soul. The LORD shall preserve thy going out and thy coming in from this time forth, and even for evermore.

**NKJV:** The LORD shall preserve you from all evil; He shall preserve your soul. The LORD shall preserve your going out and your coming in from this time forth, and even forevermore.

### Proverbs 2:7

**KJV:** He layeth up sound wisdom for the righteous: He is a buckler to them that walk uprightly.

**NKJV:** He stores up sound wisdom for the upright; He is a shield to those who walk uprightly.

### Proverbs 18:10

**KJV:** The name of the Lord is a strong tower: the righteous runneth into it, and is safe.

**NKJV:** The name of the Lord is a strong tower; the righteous run to it and are safe.

### Isaiah 54:17

**KJV:** No weapon that is formed against thee shall prosper; and every tongue that shall rise against thee in judgment thou shalt condemn. This is the heritage of the servants of the Lord, and their righteousness is of me, saith the Lord.

**NKJV:** "No weapon formed against you shall prosper, and every tongue which rises against you in judgment You shall condemn. This is the heritage of the servants of the Lord, and their righteousness is from Me," says the Lord.

### Ephesians 6:11

**KJV:** Put on the whole armour of God, that ye may be able to stand against the wiles of the devil.

**NKJV:** Put on the whole armor of God, that you may be able to stand against the wiles of the devil.

### Ephesians 6:16

**KJV:** Above all, taking the shield of faith, wherewith ye shall be able to quench all the fiery darts of the wicked.

**NKJV:** Above all, taking the shield of faith with which you will be able to quench all the fiery darts of the wicked one.

# 48 Purity

> "Thank You, Father, that today I walk in the Spirit and do not fulfill the lust of the flesh."
> Galatians 5:16

### Job 31:1

**KJV:** I made a covenant with mine eyes; why then should I think upon a maid?

**NKJV:** I have made a covenant with my eyes; why then should I look upon a young woman?

### Psalm 24:3–4

**KJV:** Who shall ascend into the hill of the Lord? Or who shall stand in his holy place? He that hath clean hands, and a pure heart; who hath not lifted up his soul unto vanity, nor sworn deceitfully.

**NKJV:** Who may ascend into the hill of the Lord? Or who may stand in His holy place? He who has clean hands and a pure heart, who has not lifted up his soul to an idol, nor sworn deceitfully.

### Daniel 1:8

**KJV:** But Daniel purposed in his heart that he would not defile himself with the portion of the king's meat, nor with the wine which he drank: therefore he requested of the prince of the eunuchs that he might not defile himself.

**NKJV:** But Daniel purposed in his heart that he would not defile himself with the portion of the king's delicacies, nor with the wine which he drank; therefore he requested of the chief of the eunuchs that he might not defile himself.

### Matthew 5:8

**KJV:** Blessed are the pure in heart: for they shall see God.

**NKJV:** Blessed are the pure in heart, for they shall see God.

### Galatians 5:16

**KJV:** This I say then, walk in the Spirit, and ye shall not fulfil the lust of the flesh.

**NKJV:** I say then: walk in the Spirit, and you shall not fulfill the lust of the flesh.

### 1 Thessalonians 4:3

**KJV:** For this is the will of God, even your sanctification, that ye should abstain from fornication.

**NKJV:** For this is the will of God, your sanctification: that you should abstain from sexual immorality.

# 49 Racism

> "Thank You, Father, that in Christ, there is neither Jew nor Greek, slave nor free, male or female, for we are all one in Christ."
> Galatians 3:28

### Mark 12:31

**KJV:** And the second is like, namely this, thou shalt love thy neighbour as thyself. There is none other commandment greater than these.

**NKJV:** And the second, like it, is this: "You shall love your neighbor as yourself." There is no other commandment greater than these.

### John 7:24

**KJV:** Judge not according to the appearance, but judge righteous judgment.

**NKJV:** Do not judge according to appearance, but judge with righteous judgment.

### Acts 10:34–36

**KJV:** Then Peter opened his mouth, and said, of a truth I perceive that God is no respecter of persons: but in every nation he that feareth him, and worketh righteousness, is accepted with him. The word which God sent unto the children of Israel, preaching peace by Jesus Christ: (he is Lord of all).

**NKJV:** Then Peter opened his mouth and said: "In truth I perceive that God shows no partiality. But in every nation whoever fears Him and works righteousness is accepted by Him. The word which God sent to the children of Israel, preaching peace through Jesus Christ—He is Lord of all."

### Acts 17:26

**KJV:** And hath made of one blood all nations of men for to dwell on all the face of the earth, and hath determined the times before appointed, and the bounds of their habitation.

**NKJV:** And He has made from one blood every nation of men to dwell on all the face of the earth, and has determined their preappointed times and the boundaries of their dwellings.

### Romans 10:12–13

**KJV:** For there is no difference between the Jew and the Greek: for the same Lord over all is rich unto all that call upon him. For whosoever shall call upon the name of the Lord shall be saved.

**NKJV:** For there is no distinction between Jew and Greek, for the same Lord over all is rich to all who call upon Him. For "whoever calls on the name of the Lord shall be saved."

## 2 Timothy 4:18

**KJV:** And the Lord shall deliver me from every evil work, and will preserve me unto his heavenly kingdom: to whom be glory for ever and ever. Amen.

**NKJV:** And the Lord will deliver me from every evil work and preserve me for His heavenly kingdom. To Him be glory forever and ever. Amen!

# Pray the Word

### Galatians 3:28

**KJV:** There is neither Jew nor Greek, there is neither bond nor free, there is neither male nor female: for ye are all one in Christ Jesus.

**NKJV:** There is neither Jew nor Greek, there is neither slave nor free, there is neither male nor female; for you are all one in Christ Jesus.

### 1 John 2:11

**KJV:** But he that hateth his brother is in darkness, and walketh in darkness, and knoweth not whither he goeth, because that darkness hath blinded his eyes.

**NKJV:** But he who hates his brother is in darkness and walks in darkness, and does not know where he is going, because the darkness has blinded his eyes.

### 1 John 3:13–16

**KJV:** Marvel not, my brethren, if the world hate you. We know that we have passed from death unto life, because we love the brethren. He that loveth not his brother abideth in death. Whosoever hateth his brother is a murderer: and ye know that no murderer hath eternal life abiding in him. Hereby perceive we the love of God, because he laid down his life for us: and we ought to lay down our lives for the brethren.

**NKJV:** Do not marvel, my brethren, if the world hates you. We know that we have passed from death to life, because we love the brethren. He who does not love his brother abides in death. Whoever hates his brother is a murderer, and you know that no murderer has eternal life abiding in him. By this we know love, because He laid down His life for us. And we also ought to lay down our lives for the brethren.

### 1 John 4:20

**KJV:** If a man say, I love God, and hateth his brother, he is a liar: for he that loveth not his brother whom he hath seen, how can he love God whom he hath not seen?

**NKJV:** If someone says, "I love God," and hates his brother, he is a liar; for he who does not love his brother whom he has seen, how can he love God whom he has not seen?

# 50 Selfishness

> "Thank You, Father, that today I look not to my own interests but the interests of others."
> 1 Corinthians 10:24

### Proverbs 11:25

**KJV:** The liberal soul shall be made fat: and he that watereth shall be watered also himself.

**NKJV:** The generous soul will be made rich, and he who waters will also be watered himself.

### Proverbs 11:26

**KJV:** He that withholdeth corn, the people shall curse him: but blessing shall be upon the head of him that selleth it.

**NKJV:** The people will curse him who withholds grain, but blessing will be on the head of him who sells it.

### Proverbs 18:1

**KJV:** Through desire a man, having separated himself, seeketh and intermeddleth with all wisdom.

**NKJV:** A man who isolates himself seeks his own desire; he rages against all wise judgment.

### Proverbs 22:9

**KJV:** He that hath a bountiful eye shall be blessed; for he giveth of his bread to the poor.

**NKJV:** He who has a generous eye will be blessed, for he gives of his bread to the poor.

### Matthew 22:35

**KJV:** Then one of them, which was a lawyer, asked him a question, tempting him, and saying, Master, which is the great commandment in the law? Jesus said unto him, Thou shalt love the Lord thy God with all thy heart, and with all thy soul, and with all thy mind. This is the first and great commandment. And the second is like unto it, Thou shalt love thy neighbour as thyself.

**NKJV:** Then one of them, a lawyer, asked Him a question, testing Him, and saying, "Teacher, which is the great commandment in the law?" Jesus said to him, "'You shall love the Lord your God with all your heart, with all your soul, and with all your mind.' This is the first and great commandment. And the second is like it: 'You shall love your neighbor as yourself.'"

### Romans 13:8–10

**KJV:** Owe no man any thing, but to love one another: for he that loveth another hath fulfilled the law. For this, thou shalt not commit adultery, thou shalt not kill, thou shalt not steal, thou shalt not bear false witness, thou shalt not covet; and if there be any other commandment, it is briefly comprehended in this saying, namely, thou shalt love thy

## Selfishness

neighbour as thyself. Love worketh no ill to his neighbour: therefore love is the fulfilling of the law.

**NKJV:** Owe no one anything except to love one another, for he who loves another has fulfilled the law. For the commandments, "You shall not commit adultery," "You shall not murder," "You shall not steal," "You shall not bear false witness," "You shall not covet," and if there is any other commandment, are all summed up in this saying, namely, "You shall love your neighbor as yourself." Love does no harm to a neighbor; therefore love is the fulfillment of the law.

### 1 Corinthians 10:24

**KJV:** Let no man seek his own, but every man another's wealth.

**NKJV:** Let no one seek his own, but each one the other's well-being.

### 2 Corinthians 5:15

**KJV:** And that he died for all, that they which live should not henceforth live unto themselves, but unto him which died for them, and rose again.

**NKJV:** And He died for all, that those who live should live no longer for themselves, but for Him who died for them and rose again.

### Philippians 2:3–4

**KJV:** Let nothing be done through strife or vainglory; but in lowliness of mind let each esteem other better than themselves. Look not every man on his own things, but every man also on the things of others.

**NKJV:** Let nothing be done through selfish ambition or conceit, but in lowliness of mind let each esteem others better than himself. Let each of you look out not only for his own interests, but also for the interests of others.

### James 3:16

**KJV:** For where envying and strife is, there is confusion and every evil work.

**NKJV:** For where envy and self-seeking exist, confusion and every evil thing are there.

# 51 Strength

> "Thank You, Father, that I can do all things through Christ who strengthens me."
> Philippians 4:13

### Nehemiah 8:10

**KJV:** Then he said unto them, Go your way, eat the fat, and drink the sweet, and send portions unto them for whom nothing is prepared: for this day is holy unto our Lord: neither be ye sorry; for the joy of the Lord is your strength.

**NKJV:** Then he said to them, "Go your way, eat the fat, drink the sweet, and send portions to those for whom nothing is prepared; for this day is holy to our Lord. Do not sorrow, for the joy of the Lord is your strength."

### Psalm 27:1

**KJV:** The Lord is my light and my salvation; whom shall I fear? The Lord is the strength of my life; of whom shall I be afraid?

**NKJV:** The Lord is my light and my salvation; whom shall I fear? The Lord is the strength of my life; of whom shall I be afraid?

### Psalm 28:7–8

**KJV:** The Lord is my strength and my shield; my heart trusted in him, and I am helped: therefore my heart greatly rejoiceth; and with my song will I praise him. The Lord is their strength, and he is the saving strength of his anointed.

**NKJV:** The Lord is my strength and my shield; my heart trusted in Him, and I am helped; therefore my heart greatly rejoices, and with my song I will praise Him. The Lord is their strength, and He is the saving refuge of His anointed.

### Psalm 84:7

**KJV:** They go from strength to strength, every one of them in Zion appeareth before God.

**NKJV:** They go from strength to strength; each one appears before God in Zion.

### Joel 3:10b

**KJV:** Let the weak say, I am strong.

**NKJV:** Let the weak say, "I am strong."

### Ephesians 6:10

**KJV:** Finally, my brethren, be strong in the Lord, and in the power of his might.

### Titus 1:15

**KJV:** Unto the pure all things are pure: but unto them that are defiled and unbelieving is nothing pure; but even their mind and conscience is defiled.

**NKJV:** To the pure all things are pure, but to those who are defiled and unbelieving nothing is pure; but even their mind and conscience are defiled.

### James 4:8

**KJV:** Draw nigh to God, and he will draw nigh to you. Cleanse your hands, ye sinners; and purify your hearts, ye double minded.

**NKJV:** Draw near to God and He will draw near to you. Cleanse your hands, you sinners; and purify your hearts, you double-minded.

### 1 John 1:5

**KJV:** This then is the message which we have heard of him, and declare unto you, that God is light, and in him is no darkness at all.

**NKJV:** This is the message which we have heard from Him and declare to you, that God is light and in Him is no darkness at all.

### 1 John 3:3

**KJV:** And every man that hath this hope in him purifieth himself, even as he is pure.

**NKJV:** And everyone who has this hope in Him purifies himself, just as He is pure.

## Pray the Word

# Strength

**NKJV:** Finally, my brethren, be strong in the Lord and in the power of His might.

### Philippians 2:13

**KJV:** For it is God which worketh in you both to will and to do of his good pleasure.

**NKJV:** For it is God who works in you both to will and to do for His good pleasure.

### Philippians 4:13

**KJV:** I can do all things through Christ which strengtheneth me.

**NKJV:** I can do all things through Christ who strengthens me.

# Pray the Word

# 52 Thankfulness

> "Thank You, Father, that in everything,
> I give thanks."
> 1 Thessalonians 5:18

### Psalm 69:30
**KJV:** I will praise the name of God with a song, and will magnify him with thanksgiving.

**NKJV:** I will praise the name of God with a song, and will magnify Him with thanksgiving.

### Psalm 95:2
**KJV:** Let us come before his presence with thanksgiving, and make a joyful noise unto him with psalms.

**NKJV:** Let us come before His presence with thanksgiving; let us shout joyfully to Him with psalms.

Pray the Word

### Psalm 100:4

**KJV:** Enter into his gates with thanksgiving, and into his courts with praise: be thankful unto him, and bless his name.

**NKJV:** Enter into His gates with thanksgiving, and into His courts with praise. Be thankful to Him, and bless His name.

### Psalm 106:1

**KJV:** Praise ye the Lord. O give thanks unto the Lord; for he is good: for his mercy endureth for ever.

**NKJV:** Praise the Lord! Oh, give thanks to the Lord, for He is good! For His mercy endures forever.

### Psalm 107:8–9

**KJV:** Oh that men would praise the Lord for his goodness, and for his wonderful works to the children of men! For he satisfieth the longing soul, and filleth the hungry soul with goodness.

**NKJV:** Oh, that men would give thanks to the Lord for His goodness, and for His wonderful works to the children of men! For He satisfies the longing soul, and fills the hungry soul with goodness.

### 2 Corinthians 4:15

**KJV:** For all things are for your sakes, that the abundant grace might through the thanksgiving of many redound to the glory of God.

**NKJV:** For all things are for your sakes, that grace, having spread through the many, may cause thanksgiving to abound to the glory of God.

### Philippians 4:6

**KJV:** Be careful for nothing; but in every thing by prayer and supplication with thanksgiving let your requests be made known unto God.

**NKJV:** Be anxious for nothing, but in everything by prayer and supplication, with thanksgiving, let your requests be made known to God.

### Colossians 3:15

**KJV:** And let the peace of God rule in your hearts, to the which also ye are called in one body; and be ye thankful.

**NKJV:** And let the peace of God rule in your hearts, to which also you were called in one body; and be thankful.

### Colossians 3:17

**KJV:** And whatsoever ye do in word or deed, do all in the name of the Lord Jesus, giving thanks to God and the Father by him.

**NKJV:** And whatever you do in word or deed, do all in the name of the Lord Jesus, giving thanks to God the Father through Him.

### Colossians 4:2

**KJV:** Continue in prayer, and watch in the same with thanksgiving.

**NKJV:** Continue earnestly in prayer, being vigilant in it with thanksgiving.

### 1 Thessalonians 5:18

**KJV:** In every thing give thanks: for this is the will of God in Christ Jesus concerning you.

**NKJV:** In everything give thanks; for this is the will of God in Christ Jesus for you.

Pray the Word

# 53

# Unsaved Loved Ones

> "Thank You, Father, that 'laborers' cross the path of my loved one. People with whom they will have a good rapport and from whom they will hear the Gospel."
> Matthew 9:37–38

### Proverbs 22:6

**KJV:** Train up a child in the way he should go: and when he is old, he will not depart from it.

**NKJV:** Train up a child in the way he should go, and when he is old he will not depart from it.

### Matthew 9:37–38

**KJV:** Then saith he unto his disciples, The harvest truly is plenteous, but the labourers are few; pray ye therefore the Lord of the harvest, that he will send forth labourers into his harvest.

**NKJV:** Then He said to His disciples, "The harvest truly is plentiful, but the laborers are few. Therefore pray the Lord of the harvest to send out laborers into His harvest."

### Luke 1:37

**KJV:** For with God nothing shall be impossible.

**NKJV:** For with God nothing will be impossible.

### Acts 16:31

**KJV:** And they said, Believe on the Lord Jesus Christ, and thou shalt be saved, and thy house.

**NKJV:** So they said, "Believe on the Lord Jesus Christ, and you will be saved, you and your household."

### Romans 8:26–27

**KJV:** Likewise the Spirit also helpeth our infirmities: for we know not what we should pray for as we ought: but the Spirit itself maketh intercession for us with groanings which cannot be uttered. And he that searcheth the hearts knoweth what is the mind of the Spirit, because he maketh intercession for the saints according to the will of God.

**NKJV:** Likewise the Spirit also helps in our weaknesses. For we do not know what we should pray for as we ought, but the Spirit Himself makes intercession for us with groanings which cannot be uttered. Now He who searches the hearts knows what the mind of the Spirit is, because He makes intercession for the saints according to the will of God.

### 2 Corinthians 4:4

**KJV:** In whom the god of this world hath blinded the minds of them which believe not, lest the light of the glorious gospel of Christ, who is the image of God, should shine unto them.

**NKJV:** Whose minds the god of this age has blinded, who do not believe, lest the light of the gospel of the glory of Christ, who is the image of God, should shine on them.

### Ephesians 1:18

**KJV:** The eyes of your understanding being enlightened; that ye may know what is the hope of his calling, and what the riches of the glory of his inheritance in the saints.

**NKJV:** The eyes of your understanding being enlightened; that you may know what is the hope of His calling, what are the riches of the glory of His inheritance in the saints.

### Ephesians 3:20

**KJV:** Now unto him that is able to do exceeding abundantly above all that we ask or think, according to the power that worketh in us.

**NKJV:** Now to Him who is able to do exceedingly abundantly above all that we ask or think, according to the power that works in us.

### Colossians 1:13

**KJV:** Who hath delivered us from the power of darkness, and hath translated us into the kingdom of his dear Son.

**NKJV:** He has delivered us from the power of darkness and conveyed us into the kingdom of the Son of His love.

### 1 Peter 3:1

**KJV:** Likewise, ye wives, be in subjection to your own husbands; that, if any obey not the word, they also may without the word be won by the conversation of the wives.

**NKJV:** Wives, likewise, be submissive to your own husbands, that even if some do not obey the word, they, without a word, may be won by the conduct of their wives.

Pray the Word

# 54 Victory

> "Thank You, Father, that today You cause me to triumph and be victorious."
> 2 Corinthians 2:14

### Genesis 50:20

**KJV:** But as for you, ye thought evil against me; but God meant it unto good, to bring to pass, as it is this day, to save much people alive.

**NKJV:** But as for you, you meant evil against me; but God meant it for good, in order to bring it about as it is this day, to save many people alive.

### Deuteronomy 23:5

**KJV:** Nevertheless the Lord thy God would not hearken unto Balaam; but the Lord thy God turned the curse into a blessing unto thee, because the Lord thy God loved thee.

NKJV: Nevertheless the LORD your God would not listen to Balaam, but the LORD your God turned the curse into a blessing for you, because the LORD your God loves you.

### Deuteronomy 30:19

KJV: I call heaven and earth to record this day against you, that I have set before you life and death, blessing and cursing: therefore choose life, that both thou and thy seed may live.

NKJV: I call heaven and earth as witnesses today against you, that I have set before you life and death, blessing and cursing; therefore choose life, that both you and your descendants may live.

### 2 Chronicles 20:15b

KJV: Thus saith the LORD unto you, Be not afraid nor dismayed by reason of this great multitude; for the battle is not yours, but God's.

NKJV: Thus says the LORD to you: "Do not be afraid nor dismayed because of this great multitude, for the battle is not yours, but God's."

### Psalm 34:19

KJV: Many are the afflictions of the righteous: but the LORD delivereth him out of them all.

NKJV: Many are the afflictions of the righteous, but the LORD delivers him out of them all.

### Psalm 118:6

KJV: The LORD is on my side; I will not fear. what can man do unto me?

NKJV: The LORD is on my side; I will not fear. What can man do to me?

### Proverbs 21:31

**KJV:** The horse is prepared against the day of battle: but safety is of the LORD.

**NKJV:** The horse is prepared for the day of battle, but deliverance is of the LORD.

### Romans 8:31

**KJV:** What shall we then say to these things? If God be for us, who can be against us?

**NKJV:** What then shall we say to these things? If God is for us, who can be against us?

### Romans 8:37

**KJV:** Nay, in all these things we are more than conquerors through him that loved us.

**NKJV:** Yet in all these things we are more than conquerors through Him who loved us.

### 1 Corinthians 15:57

**KJV:** But thanks be to God, which giveth us the victory through our Lord Jesus Christ.

**NKJV:** But thanks be to God, who gives us the victory through our Lord Jesus Christ.

### 2 Corinthians 1:20

**KJV:** For all the promises of God in him are yea, and in him Amen, unto the glory of God by us.

**NKJV:** For all the promises of God in Him are Yes, and in Him Amen, to the glory of God through us.

### 2 Corinthians 2:14a

**KJV:** Now thanks be unto God, which always causeth us to triumph in Christ.

**NKJV:** Now thanks be to God who always leads us in triumph in Christ.

### 2 Peter 1:2–4

**KJV:** Grace and peace be multiplied unto you through the knowledge of God, and of Jesus our Lord, according as his divine power hath given unto us all things that pertain unto life and godliness, through the knowledge of him that hath called us to glory and virtue: whereby are given unto us exceeding great and precious promises: that by these ye might be partakers of the divine nature, having escaped the corruption that is in the world through lust.

**NKJV:** Grace and peace be multiplied to you in the knowledge of God and of Jesus our Lord, as His divine power has given to us all things that pertain to life and godliness, through the knowledge of Him who called us by glory and virtue, by which have been given to us exceedingly great and precious promises, that through these you may be partakers of the divine nature, having escaped the corruption that is in the world through lust.

### 1 John 4:4

**KJV:** Ye are of God, little children, and have overcome them: because greater is he that is in you, than he that is in the world.

**NKJV:** You are of God, little children, and have overcome them, because He who is in you is greater than he who is in the world.

### 1 John 5:4

**KJV:** For whatsoever is born of God overcometh the world: and this is the victory that overcometh the world, even our faith.

**NKJV:** For whatever is born of God overcomes the world. And this is the victory that has overcome the world—our faith.

## Pray the Word

# 55 What's Taking So Long, God?

> "Thank You, Father, that today
> I hold fast to my profession of faith
> without wavering."
> Hebrews 10:23

### 1 Kings 8:56

**KJV:** Blessed be the Lord, that hath given rest unto his people Israel, according to all that he promised: there hath not failed one word of all his good promise, which he promised by the hand of Moses his servant.

**NKJV:** Blessed be the Lord, who has given rest to His people Israel, according to all that He promised. There has not failed one word of all His good promise, which He promised through His servant Moses.

## Pray the Word

### Psalm 62:5

**KJV:** My soul, wait thou only upon God; for my expectation is from him.

**NKJV:** My soul, wait silently for God alone, for my expectation is from Him.

### Psalm 89:33

**KJV:** Nevertheless my lovingkindness will I not utterly take from him, nor suffer my faithfulness to fail.

**NKJV:** Nevertheless My lovingkindness I will not utterly take from him, nor allow My faithfulness to fail.

### Psalm 119:89

**KJV:** For ever, O LORD, thy word is settled in heaven.

**NKJV:** Forever, O LORD, your word is settled in heaven.

### Isaiah 55:11

**KJV:** So shall my word be that goeth forth out of my mouth: it shall not return unto me void, but it shall accomplish that which I please, and it shall prosper in the thing whereto I sent it.

**NKJV:** So shall My word be that goes forth from My mouth; it shall not return to Me void, but it shall accomplish what I please, and it shall prosper in the thing for which I sent it.

### Jeremiah 1:12

**KJV:** Then said the LORD unto me, Thou hast well seen: for I will hasten my word to perform it.

**NKJV:** Then the LORD said to me, "You have seen well, for I am ready to perform My word."

### Mark 4:26–29

**KJV:** And he said, So is the kingdom of God, as if a man should cast seed into the ground; and should sleep, and rise night and day, and the seed should spring and grow up, he knoweth not how. For the earth bringeth forth fruit of herself; first the blade, then the ear, after that the full corn in the ear. But when the fruit is brought forth, immediately he putteth in the sickle, because the harvest is come.

**NKJV:** And He said, "The kingdom of God is as if a man should scatter seed on the ground, and should sleep by night and rise by day, and the seed should sprout and grow, he himself does not know how. For the earth yields crops by itself: first the blade, then the head, after that the full grain in the head. But when the grain ripens, immediately he puts in the sickle, because the harvest has come."

### Luke 21:19

**KJV:** In your patience possess ye your souls.

**NKJV:** By your patience possess your souls.

### Luke 21:33

**KJV:** Heaven and earth shall pass away: but my words shall not pass away.

**NKJV:** Heaven and earth will pass away, but My words will by no means pass away.

### Acts 20:24

**KJV:** But none of these things move me, neither count I my life dear unto myself, so that I might finish my course with joy, and the ministry, which I have received of the Lord Jesus, to testify the gospel of the grace of God.

**NKJV:** But none of these things move me; nor do I count my life dear to myself, so that I may finish my race with joy, and the ministry which I received from the Lord Jesus, to testify to the gospel of the grace of God.

### Acts 27:25

**KJV:** Wherefore, sirs, be of good cheer: for I believe God, that it shall be even as it was told me.

**NKJV:** Therefore take heart, men, for I believe God that it will be just as it was told me.

### Romans 3:4

**KJV:** God forbid: yea, let God be true, but every man a liar; as it is written, That thou mightest be justified in thy sayings, and mightest overcome when thou art judged.

**NKJV:** Certainly not! Indeed, let God be true but every man a liar. As it is written: "That You may be justified in Your words, and may overcome when You are judged."

### 2 Corinthians 4:17–18

**KJV:** For our light affliction, which is but for a moment, worketh for us a far more exceeding and eternal weight of glory; while we look not at the things which are seen, but at the things which are not seen: for the things which are seen are temporal; but the things which are not seen are eternal.

**NKJV:** For our light affliction, which is but for a moment, is working for us a far more exceeding and eternal weight of glory, while we do not look at the things which are seen, but at the things which are not seen. For the things which are seen are temporary, but the things which are not seen are eternal.

### 2 Corinthians 5:7

**KJV:** For we walk by faith, not by sight.

**NKJV:** For we walk by faith, not by sight.

### Galatians 6:9

**KJV:** And let us not be weary in well doing: for in due season we shall reap, if we faint not.

**NKJV:** And let us not grow weary while doing good, for in due season we shall reap if we do not lose heart.

### Ephesians 3:20

**KJV:** Now unto him that is able to do exceeding abundantly above all that we ask or think, according to the power that worketh in us.

**NKJV:** Now to Him who is able to do exceedingly abundantly above all that we ask or think, according to the power that works in us.

### Hebrews 4:14

**KJV:** Seeing then that we have a great high priest, that is passed into the heavens, Jesus the Son of God, let us hold fast our profession.

**NKJV:** Seeing then that we have a great High Priest who has passed through the heavens, Jesus the Son of God, let us hold fast our confession.

### Hebrews 6:12

**KJV:** That ye be not slothful, but followers of them who through faith and patience inherit the promises.

**NKJV:** That you do not become sluggish, but imitate those who through faith and patience inherit the promises.

## Pray the Word

### Hebrews 10:23

**KJV:** Let us hold fast the profession of our faith without wavering; (for he is faithful that promised).

**NKJV:** Let us hold fast the confession of our hope without wavering, for He who promised is faithful.

### Hebrews 10:35–36

**KJV:** Cast not away therefore your confidence, which hath great recompence of reward. For ye have need of patience, that, after ye have done the will of God, ye might receive the promise.

**NKJV:** Therefore do not cast away your confidence, which has great reward. For you have need of endurance, so that after you have done the will of God, you may receive the promise.

### Hebrews 11:1

**KJV:** Now faith is the substance of things hoped for, the evidence of things not seen.

**NKJV:** Now faith is the substance of things hoped for, the evidence of things not seen.

### Hebrews 12:1–3

**KJV:** Wherefore seeing we also are compassed about with so great a cloud of witnesses, let us lay aside every weight, and the sin which doth so easily beset us, and let us run with patience the race that is set before us, looking unto Jesus the author and finisher of our faith; who for the joy that was set before him endured the cross, despising the shame, and is set down at the right hand of the throne of God. For consider him that endured such contradiction of sinners against himself, lest ye be wearied and faint in your minds.

**NKJV:** Therefore we also, since we are surrounded by so great a cloud of witnesses, let us lay aside every weight, and the sin which so easily ensnares us, and let us run with endurance the race that is set before us, looking unto Jesus, the author and finisher of our faith, who for the joy that was set before Him endured the cross, despising the shame, and has sat down at the right hand of the throne of God. For consider Him who endured such hostility from sinners against Himself, lest you become weary and discouraged in your souls.

### James 1:2–4

**KJV:** My brethren, count it all joy when ye fall into divers temptations; knowing this, that the trying of your faith worketh patience. But let patience have her perfect work, that ye may be perfect and entire, wanting nothing.

**NKJV:** My brethren, count it all joy when you fall into various trials, knowing that the testing of your faith produces patience But let patience have its perfect work, that you may be perfect and complete, lacking nothing.

Pray the Word

# 56

# Who You Are in Christ

> "Thank You, Father, that I am the righteousness of God in Christ."
> 2 Corinthians 5:21

### John 1:12

**KJV:** But as many as received him, to them gave he power to become the sons of God, even to them that believe on his name.

**NKJV:** But as many as received Him, to them He gave the right to become children of God, to those who believe in His name.

### Romans 3:24

**KJV:** Being justified freely by his grace through the redemption that is in Christ Jesus.

**NKJV:** Being justified freely by His grace through the redemption that is in Christ Jesus.

### Romans 5:1

**KJV:** Therefore being justified by faith, we have peace with God through our Lord Jesus Christ.

**NKJV:** Therefore, having been justified by faith, we have peace with God through our Lord Jesus Christ.

### Romans 5:9

**KJV:** Much more then, being now justified by his blood, we shall be saved from wrath through him.

**NKJV:** Much more then, having now been justified by His blood, we shall be saved from wrath through Him.

### Romans 8:1

**KJV:** There is therefore now no condemnation to them which are in Christ Jesus, who walk not after the flesh, but after the Spirit.

**NKJV:** There is therefore now no condemnation to those who are in Christ Jesus, who do not walk according to the flesh, but according to the Spirit.

### Romans 8:15

**KJV:** For ye have not received the spirit of bondage again to fear; but ye have received the Spirit of adoption, whereby we cry, Abba, Father.

**NKJV:** For you did not receive the spirit of bondage again to fear, but you received the Spirit of adoption by whom we cry out, "Abba, Father."

### 1 Corinthians 1:30

**KJV:** But of him are ye in Christ Jesus, who of God is made unto us wisdom, and righteousness, and sanctification, and redemption.

**NKJV:** But of Him you are in Christ Jesus, who became for us wisdom from God—and righteousness and sanctification and redemption.

### 2 Corinthians 2:14

**KJV:** Now thanks be unto God, which always causeth us to triumph in Christ, and maketh manifest the savour of his knowledge by us in every place.

**NKJV:** Now thanks be to God who always leads us in triumph in Christ, and through us diffuses the fragrance of His knowledge in every place.

### 2 Corinthians 5:17

**KJV:** Therefore if any man be in Christ, he is a new creature: old things are passed away; behold, all things are become new.

**NKJV:** Therefore, if anyone is in Christ, he is a new creation; old things have passed away; behold, all things have become new.

### 2 Corinthians 5:21

**KJV:** For he hath made him to be sin for us, who knew no sin; that we might be made the righteousness of God in him.

**NKJV:** For He made Him who knew no sin to be sin for us, that we might become the righteousness of God in Him.

### Galatians 3:28

**KJV:** There is neither Jew nor Greek, there is neither bond nor free, there is neither male nor female: for ye are all one in Christ Jesus.

**NKJV:** There is neither Jew nor Greek, there is neither slave nor free, there is neither male nor female; for you are all one in Christ Jesus.

## Pray the Word

### Ephesians 1:3

**KJV:** Blessed be the God and Father of our Lord Jesus Christ, who hath blessed us with all spiritual blessings in heavenly places in Christ.

**NKJV:** Blessed be the God and Father of our Lord Jesus Christ, who has blessed us with every spiritual blessing in the heavenly places in Christ.

### Ephesians 1:4–7

**KJV:** According as he hath chosen us in him before the foundation of the world, that we should be holy and without blame before him in love: having predestinated us unto the adoption of children by Jesus Christ to himself, according to the good pleasure of his will, to the praise of the glory of his grace, wherein he hath made us accepted in the beloved. In whom we have redemption through his blood, the forgiveness of sins, according to the riches of his grace.

**NKJV:** Just as He chose us in Him before the foundation of the world, that we should be holy and without blame before Him in love, having predestined us to adoption as sons by Jesus Christ to Himself, according to the good pleasure of His will, to the praise of the glory of His grace, by which He made us accepted in the Beloved. In Him we have redemption through His blood, the forgiveness of sins, according to the riches of His grace.

### Ephesians 2:6

**KJV:** And hath raised us up together, and made us sit together in heavenly places in Christ Jesus.

**NKJV:** And raised us up together, and made us sit together in the heavenly places in Christ Jesus.

### Colossians 2:10

**KJV:** And ye are complete in him, which is the head of all principality and power.

**NKJV:** And you are complete in Him, who is the head of all principality and power.

### 1 Peter 2:5

**KJV:** Ye also, as lively stones, are built up a spiritual house, an holy priesthood, to offer up spiritual sacrifices, acceptable to God by Jesus Christ.

**NKJV:** You also, as living stones, are being built up a spiritual house, a holy priesthood, to offer up spiritual sacrifices acceptable to God through Jesus Christ.

### 1 Peter 2:9

**KJV:** But ye are a chosen generation, a royal priesthood, an holy nation, a peculiar people; that ye should shew forth the praises of him who hath called you out of darkness into his marvellous light.

**NKJV:** But you are a chosen generation, a royal priesthood, a holy nation, His own special people, that you may proclaim the praises of Him who called you out of darkness into His marvelous light.

### 1 John 3:2a

**KJV:** Beloved, now are we the sons of God.

**NKJV:** Beloved, now we are children of God.

### Revelation 1:6

**KJV:** And hath made us kings and priests unto God and his Father; to him be glory and dominion for ever and ever. Amen.

**NKJV:** And has made us kings and priests to His God and Father, to Him be glory and dominion forever and ever. Amen.

Pray the Word

# 57 Wisdom

> "Thank You, Father, that today I have wisdom from God liberally."
> James 1:5

### Psalm 90:12

**KJV:** So teach us to number our days, that we may apply our hearts unto wisdom.

**NKJV:** So teach us to number our days, that we may gain a heart of wisdom.

### Proverbs 1:7

**KJV:** The fear of the LORD is the beginning of knowledge: but fools despise wisdom and instruction.

**NKJV:** The fear of the LORD is the beginning of knowledge, but fools despise wisdom and instruction.

# Pray the Word

### Proverbs 3:13–18

**KJV:** Happy is the man that findeth wisdom, and the man that getteth understanding. For the merchandise of it is better than the merchandise of silver, and the gain thereof than fine gold. She is more precious than rubies: and all the things thou canst desire are not to be compared unto her. length of days is in her right hand; and in her left hand riches and honour. Her ways are ways of pleasantness, and all her paths are peace. She is a tree of life to them that lay hold upon her: and happy is every one that retaineth her.

**NKJV:** Happy is the man who finds wisdom, and the man who gains understanding; for her proceeds are better than the profits of silver, and her gain than fine gold. She is more precious than rubies, and all the things you may desire cannot compare with her. Length of days is in her right hand, in her left hand riches and honor. Her ways are ways of pleasantness, and all her paths are peace. She is a tree of life to those who take hold of her, and happy are all who retain her.

### Proverbs 4:7–8

**KJV:** Wisdom is the principal thing; therefore get wisdom: and with all thy getting get understanding. Exalt her, and she shall promote thee: she shall bring thee to honour, when thou dost embrace her.

**NKJV:** Wisdom is the principal thing; therefore get wisdom. And in all your getting, get understanding. Exalt her, and she will promote you; she will bring you honor, when you embrace her.

### Proverbs 11:2

**KJV:** When pride cometh, then cometh shame: but with the lowly is wisdom.

**NKJV:** When pride comes, then comes shame; but with the humble is wisdom.

Wisdom

### Proverbs 12:15

**KJV:** The way of a fool is right in his own eyes: but he that hearkeneth unto counsel is wise.

**NKJV:** The way of a fool is right in his own eyes, but he who heeds counsel is wise.

### Proverbs 16:16

**KJV:** How much better is it to get wisdom than gold! And to get understanding rather to be chosen than silver!

**NKJV:** How much better to get wisdom than gold! And to get understanding is to be chosen rather than silver.

### Proverbs 19:8

**KJV:** He that getteth wisdom loveth his own soul: he that keepeth understanding shall find good.

**NKJV:** He who gets wisdom loves his own soul; he who keeps understanding will find good.

### Proverbs 24:3–7

**KJV:** Through wisdom is an house builded; and by understanding it is established: and by knowledge shall the chambers be filled with all precious and pleasant riches. A wise man is strong; yea, a man of knowledge increaseth strength. For by wise counsel thou shalt make thy war: and in multitude of counsellors there is safety. Wisdom is too high for a fool: he openeth not his mouth in the gate.

**NKJV:** Through wisdom a house is built, and by understanding it is established; by knowledge the rooms are filled with all precious and pleasant riches. A wise man is strong, yes, a man of knowledge increases strength; for by wise counsel you will wage your own war, and in a multitude of counselors there is safety. Wisdom is too lofty for a fool; he does not open his mouth in the gate.

# Pray the Word

### Matthew 7:24

**KJV:** Therefore whosoever heareth these sayings of mine, and doeth them, I will liken him unto a wise man, which built his house upon a rock.

**NKJV:** Therefore whoever hears these sayings of Mine, and does them, I will liken him to a wise man who built his house on the rock.

### Colossians 3:16

**KJV:** Let the word of Christ dwell in you richly in all wisdom; teaching and admonishing one another in psalms and hymns and spiritual songs, singing with grace in your hearts to the Lord.

**NKJV:** Let the word of Christ dwell in you richly in all wisdom, teaching and admonishing one another in psalms and hymns and spiritual songs, singing with grace in your hearts to the Lord.

### Colossians 4:5–6

**KJV:** Walk in wisdom toward them that are without, redeeming the time. Let your speech be alway with grace, seasoned with salt, that ye may know how ye ought to answer every man.

**NKJV:** Walk in wisdom toward those who are outside, redeeming the time. Let your speech always be with grace, seasoned with salt, that you may know how you ought to answer each one.

### 1 Corinthians 1:30

**KJV:** But of him are ye in Christ Jesus, who of God is made unto us wisdom, and righteousness, and sanctification, and redemption.

**NKJV:** But of Him you are in Christ Jesus, who became for us wisdom from God—and righteousness and sanctification and redemption.

# Wisdom

### James 1:5

**KJV:** If any of you lack wisdom, let him ask of God, that giveth to all men liberally, and upbraideth not; and it shall be given him.

**NKJV:** If any of you lacks wisdom, let him ask of God, who gives to all liberally and without reproach, and it will be given to him.

### James 3:17

**KJV:** But the wisdom that is from above is first pure, then peaceable, gentle, and easy to be intreated, full of mercy and good fruits, without partiality, and without hypocrisy.

**NKJV:** But the wisdom that is from above is first pure, then peaceable, gentle, willing to yield, full of mercy and good fruits, without partiality and without hypocrisy.

# HOW TO START THE MOST IMPORTANT RELATIONSHIP OF YOUR LIFE

Shark fishing is my hobby. I use a kayak to paddle my bait hundreds of yards into the ocean, then paddle back and fish from the shore. Some time ago, I was in the middle of a four-hour battle with a very large shark, and a crowd had gathered from around the beach to see what I was going to reel in. A man in the crowd struck up a conversation with me while I was battling this shark. He asked me what I did for a living, and I told him I was a pastor.

When people discover that I am pastor, I get a variety of responses. This man's response was unusual. He simply blurted out with disdain, "Well, I hate organized religion!" I replied, "Me too." He was surprised at my reply, so I continued, asking, "Do you know who else hates organized religion?" Before he could respond, I shocked him further and said, "Jesus!" Now, I had this fellow's undivided attention, and I hope that I now have yours as well.

You see, Christianity is not about religion. It is about a relationship with a loving, heavenly Father through His one Son, Jesus Christ. I believe that you have a figurative homing beacon on the inside of you, placed there by the God who created you. It is a spiritual hole, if you will, that can only be filled by the very same God.

I understand this personally. Before I entered into a relationship with Jesus, I tried to fill that hole with women, alcohol, and fighting. It was fun for a while, but when the fun was over, and the things I tried to fill that vacuum with came crashing down around me, I still had that homing beacon on the inside of me—my heavenly Father gently, patiently, and ever so lovingly calling me home.

Maybe you can sense the emptiness on the inside of you and the loving call of your heavenly Father, imploring you to come home.

Why not surrender your life to Him and find the joy, peace, and purpose you've been looking for all your life? Why not start the most important relationship of your life? It's so simple, but life transforming.

Please pray this prayer with me. Repeat it out loud, but mean it from your heart. I discovered a long time ago that when you reach out to God from your heart, He will always reach back to you with His love.

Pray this simple prayer with me now:

> *"Father God, I come to You now. Sin, I turn my back on you. Jesus, I turn to You now. I believe you were raised from the dead just for me. Come into my heart, and be my Lord. I surrender my life to You today. I enter into a relationship with You today!"*

If you prayed that prayer, please contact us here at Joy Church, and let us know that you started the most important relationship of your life. We want to respect your privacy and dignity, but we also want to give you some information to help you walk out this new relationship in a life-giving way!

You can email us at mail@joychurchinternational.org or give us a call at 615-773-5252. You can write to us at Joy Church, P.O. Box 247, Mount Juliet, TN, 37121.

If you live in or are visiting the Nashville/Mount Juliet, TN area, we would love to invite you to join us for one of our upcoming services. For more information and directions, please visit our website at www.joychurch.net. We look forward to hearing from you!

Please remember that God loves you as if you were the only person in this world to love!

Jim Frease and his wife, Anne, and their son, Johnathan.

# ABOUT THE AUTHOR

Jim Frease is the founder and senior pastor of Joy Church in Mt. Juliet, Tennessee, and founder and president of World Changers Bible Institute (WCBI).

He is also the founder of Joy Ministerial Exchange (JME), a ministerial organization designed to impart wisdom to pastors across the country.

Jim emphasizes a relationship with Jesus Christ, not religion; the Word of God, not tradition; and he emphasizes enjoying life, not enduring it. He teaches not just what to do, but how.

Jim and his wife, Anne, have been married since 1990, and they deeply love their son, Johnathan. Jim loves spending time with his family, and he enjoys Ohio State football and fishing. Anne loves to shop. Sometimes, they compromise and shop at Bass Pro Shops®.

Most importantly, Jim and Anne are deeply in love with the Lord Jesus Christ and are completely committed to His Word. As they minister, they do so with humor & joy (Neh. 8:10) and integrity (Ps. 26:11), propelling the listener to a greater intimacy with Jesus.

# ABOUT JOY CHURCH

Based out of Mt. Juliet, Tennessee,
Joy Church is a rapidly growing, multigenerational,
multicultural church with people from almost every
denominational background—including those with
no church background at all.

At Joy Church, we don't believe in organized religion;
we believe in organized relationship with God the Father
through His Son, Jesus Christ.

We are not about tradition but the liberating Word of God.
We are not about enduring life—we are about enjoying life!

For more information, please visit joychurch.net